Chung · Hyo · Ye

Tales of filial devotion, loyalty, respect and benevolence

from the history and folklore of Korea

Front cover: image of a heavenly being offering an incense burner to the Buddha.
Taken from the Sacred Bell of King Seongdeok (cast AD 771),
"the world's most beautiful bell" in the view of many artists worldwide.

Published by Korean Spirit and Culture Promotion Project
Publisher Kim Jae-Woong
Editorial Supervision Soon-Young Lee
Editorial Board Lee Ji-Seon, Han Yoon-Sang, Chang Hang-Jin, Matthew Jackson
Printed and Bound by Samjung Munhwasa
Chungjeong-ro 37-18, Seodaemun-gu, Seoul

First edition, August 2006
Revised Edition, August 2017

ISBN: 0-9779613-9-7

When you have read this booklet, please donate it to a library or
school so that it can be shared with others. Thank you.

Contents

Chapter 3 Wu-ae: Fraternal Love

Chapter 4 Ye: A Virtuous Way of Life

Preface

Korea is a nation that has always loved peace and has done everything in its power to preserve it. Based on the teachings of *Hongik Ingan,* which means one should "live and act for the benefit of all mankind," reverence for the Heavens and respect for human life is deeply rooted in the spirit of the Korean people.

Traditionally, large family households consisting of more than three generations were very common in Korean society. Within these large families, elder family members looked after younger family members, and children learned to treat their elders with respect. They also learned to put the interests of others first and take care of their younger siblings. Such an upbringing serves as the basis for an attitude that places the good of one's neighbor and society above one's own. It also serves as a foundation for the willingness to sacrifice oneself for one's country.

This book is a collection of stories about love and devotion, many of which are taken directly from historical records, and some classic folktales. They are stories about awareness of one's roots, about love for parents based on the spirit that puts "us" before "me," about love between siblings, and about love of one's country and one's people.

Timeline of Korean History

BC 700000~BC 80000	Paleolithic Period
BC 8000~BC 2000	Neolithic Period
BC 2333~BC 108	Old Choson Dynasty: The First Kingdom of Korea (Bronze Age & Iron Age)
BC 57~AD 668	Three Kingdoms Period: Koguryo, Paekche and Silla
668	Three Kingdoms unified under Silla
668~ 935	Unified Silla
918~1392	Koryo Dynasty
1392~ 1910	Choson Dynasty
1910~1945	Japanese Occupation
1948	Korea divided into North (DPRK) and South (ROK)
1950~1953	Korean War
1986	South Korea hosts Asian Games in Seoul
1988	South Korea hosts Summer Olympic Games in Seoul
1995	South Korea joins OECD
2002	South Korea and Japan Co-host 2002 FIFA World Cup
2005	South Korea hosts APEC Summit in Busan
2010	South Korea hosts G20 Summit in Seoul

Chapter 1

Hyo: Filial Devotion

Love of Lotus Flower Pavilion of Changdok Palace

Built in the 15th century, UNESCO's World Cultural Heritage

Under the Burning Sun

A brush seller once arrived in a village, and went to the village school to sell his wares. When he got there, he found several young children reading books on the veranda of the schoolhouse. Most of the children were in the shade, but one child was sitting reading his book under the burning sun. The man thought this strange, and asked the boy,

"How old are you?"

"I am seven years old," the boy replied.

"Why are you reading under the sun, while other students are on the cool floor?"

The boy, wiping the sweat from his forehead, answered,

"My family is poor, and my father works as a day laborer[1] in order to pay my school fees. My books, brushes, and papers are all the result of my father's hard work and sweat. I feel guilty reading on the cool floor while my father is working in a field in the summer heat. That is why I am reading this book under the burning sun."

Deeply moved, the brush-seller praised the boy for his thoughtfulness towards his father, and gave him his best brushes as a reward.

---

[1] Because his father did not own his own land, he worked for other farmers in return for a wage.

The Poor Scholar and the Minister's Daughter

In Choson Korea (1392~1910), there was once a government minister who had a beautiful daughter. When she came of age, the minister began to look for an intelligent young man to be her husband. Shortly afterwards, a young scholar came to see the minister to seek his daughter's hand in marriage. The minister, seeing his poor and shabby appearance, refused him immediately.

However, as it was just past midday, he asked the young man to stay for lunch, and had a table prepared for him, laden with sumptuous dishes and expensive wines.

The poor scholar's eyes opened wide at the sight of delicacies, which he had never eaten or even seen before. However, he did not eat, but began to wrap up the food and put it in a bag he was carrying.

Greatly surprised, the minister asked the young scholar why he was storing the food away instead of eating it.

The young man replied, "I have never seen such fine dishes before, and so I am taking them home to give to my mother."

The minister, deeply touched by the man's devotion, instantly changed his mind and gave him permission to marry his daughter. The young scholar was the famous Yi Wonik[2] (1547~1634), and went on to become a government minister like his father-in-law.

---

[2] In Korean, a surname normally comes before the given name. Names in this book follow this convention.

A Visit to Seoul

Some hundreds of years ago, a young scholar who lived in a remote village married a woman from Kwachon. After the wedding ceremony, he went to live with the bride's family. His father, worried about his son, said to him, "There is only one hill separating Kwachon and Seoul. When you arrive in Kwachon, you must take care never to visit Seoul."

"Why not, father?" the young scholar asked.

"If you set eyes on a bustling, flourishing capital city, your mind will become unstable and you will be unable to concentrate on your studies. Please promise that you will remember this."

The scholar was a devoted son, and he always did whatever his father asked of him. Therefore, he promised that he would follow his instructions, and left for his wife's house.

After he had been living there for some time, however, it occurred to him that it would be a shame not to go and visit Seoul, since it was so close by. He felt that if he did not go and see Seoul then, he would be unlikely to have the chance to do so in the future. Therefore, in spite of his father's advice, he climbed over the hill and made his way to Seoul.

Once on the other side, however, he felt so uncomfortable going against his father's wishes that he turned back to Kwachon after reaching the South Gate.

When he returned to his wife's house, however, he reasoned with himself that it would be acceptable for him to go Seoul provided that he could keep it a secret from his father. Again, on the next day, he made his way as far as the

South Gate. However, he again remembered what his father had said to him, and being unable to pass further, went back to his wife's house.

He repeated this several times, going to the South Gate in the morning and then returning to Kwachon. A soldier on guard at the gate thought the scholar's actions suspicious and reported him to the authorities. He was arrested and interrogated by the head of the police.

"Why do you appear at the South Gate every day? What are you planning to do?"

The timid scholar replied in a faltering voice.

"I recently moved to Kwachon after getting married, and had never been so close to Seoul before. It was my father's words that made me behave in this way."

"Your father's words? Explain what you mean."

The scholar related the whole story, and begged the officer to pardon him.

"Since I could neither break my promise to my father nor abandon my wish to see Seoul, I walked back and forth in front of the South Gate every day."

The officer saw that the scholar was a devoted son, and said, "Unless you yourself had told your father, nobody would have known about your coming to Seoul. But you kept your promise nevertheless, out of devotion to your parents. This is conduct worthy of a true son, and you deserve to be rewarded. Since you are already in Seoul, please take the opportunity to see the city, and then go back to your hometown."

The young scholar was rewarded by the officer and taken on a tour of the city by a military escort, before returning home to his wife. He eventually told his father what had happened, and related all he had seen in detail. Later, he passed the state examination and rose to become prime minister.

My Mother's Troubles

Once, in a village, there lived a lazy delinquent. Having lost his father at a young age, he had been raised by his widowed mother, and had started to go astray early on in life. He never listened to his mother's words, and was always causing mischief and disturbing the lives of the villagers.

His mother was very worried for his future, and called him to her one day, saying,

"I cannot allow you to live like this anymore. Fortunately, I have heard that there is a scholar of some reputation who is now living in the village. You must go and study under him."

The mother took her son to see the scholar. At first, the scholar tried to teach him to study books and the teachings of the sages. However, the boy showed no signs of progress.

One day, the scholar said to him,

"The weather today is very hot. On a day like this, the best thing for us to do is to find a stream where we can bathe our feet. Also, we can eat watermelon and gold melon, having cooled them in the stream. Let us go now."

The excited student rushed to get ready. The teacher told the boy to take the fruit, giving him a large watermelon and ten gold melons to carry. Pleased to be going on a trip, the student held tightly on to them, and hurried on his way.

But before they had walked one *majang* (about 400m), the boy began to sweat in the summer heat. His steps became unsteady, and he was on the verge of falling over. Unable to endure the heat, he said to his teacher,

"I cannot go any further. Let us rest here for a while, and then go back home."

Hearing this, the teacher scolded the boy,

"You are complaining about walking only this far, carrying a watermelon? Think how your mother carried you for ten months, how she worked all day weaving cloth and tending to the farm with a heavy baby in her womb."

At that moment, the boy felt a sharp pain, as if something was piercing his chest. Still holding the watermelon, he looked up at the sky, and soon tears started to pour from his eyes. He knelt before his teacher and said,

"Teacher, I have been so foolish. I repent from the bottom of my heart."

A Mother's Love

There was once a wicked son who lived with his widowed mother. The older she became, the wearier he grew of taking care of her.

One day, the son said to his mother in a gentle voice,

"Mother, would you like to go to the river with me today?"

"Of course!" his mother replied, delighted.

"The fish in the river are really beautiful to see," said the son, who was in fact planning to abandon his aged mother.

They made their way towards the river, and when he had brought her to the river's edge, the son pointed to the deep water and said,

"Look beneath the surface. Can you see many fish?"

As soon as she stepped into the river and leaned over to peer at the fish, the son immediately let go of her hand. The mother, however, instinctively grabbed on to her son's clothing. At that moment, a scholar who was passing by and had witnessed this came running over.

"Look here! What were you trying to do?" he shouted at the son, intending to hit him with his fist. At that moment, the mother stepped in between her son and the scholar and said to him indignantly,

"Leave him alone! What did my son do wrong that you should try to hit him?"

Confused, the scholar replied, "Wasn't he about to push you into the river?"

The woman took her son's hand and replied,

"You are mistaken. In fact, I was about to throw myself into the river, but my son rushed all the way from home to stop me."

The son could only lower his head in shame, and the scholar could not say anything.

The True Practice of Hyo

Han Seokbong (1543~1605) was born in Kaesong during the Choson Dynasty, in the reign of King Sonjo. His father had passed away when he was young, and he grew up in poverty with his widowed mother. Despite being very poor, his mother made a living by selling rice cakes, and was thus able to support her son in his studies.

As Seokbong grew older and began to study more seriously, his mother began to save even more, and used the money she saved to buy him ink and paper. Seokbong, as a dutiful son, devoted himself to his studies in order to repay his mother's care. However, to ease the burden his mother had placed on herself, he did not use the paper and ink she had bought for him, but practiced brush writing with water on the surfaces of jars instead, or on stones and leaves.

One day, Seokbong realized that his mother was starving herself in order to save money for ink and paper. With an ache in his heart, he said to her, "Mother, there is still paper left. You do not have to buy any more."

She replied, "If there is paper left, it shows that you have been lazy in your studies."

After being scolded like this, Seokbong told her the truth. But his mother said to him in an even sterner voice, "You do not know the true meaning of devotion to your mother. My sincere hope for you is that you will concentrate on study and make yourself a better person. Since buying paper and ink for you is the only pleasure I have, what does it matter if I have to starve? Why do you not understand my intention?"

Seokbong, shocked and moved by her words, left for a temple in order to study calligraphy more seriously.[3] His talents were soon recognized by his teachers, and his work was greatly admired.

After three years had passed, Seokbong was unable to stay at the temple any longer. Whenever he thought of his mother, who became a widow at a young age, and sacrificed everything to support her only son, his heart felt as though it was being torn apart. Moreover, he had become so accomplished at brush writing that there was no longer anyone in the temple from whom he could learn. He considered that his studies had progressed far enough, and so he left for home.

It was dark when he arrived, and his mother was cutting rice cakes in the house under a dim light. Seokbong was so full of joy that he opened the door wide and immediately entered the room. His mother, however, appeared less than pleased to see him there. Calmly, and somewhat coldly, she asked him,

"Have you completed your studies?"

"Yes mother, I have."

"Let us see how well you have done."

His mother placed paper and ink in front of Seokbong and some uncut rice cakes in front of herself.

"You will write characters and I will cut cakes, and we will see who is better."

His mother then blew out the lamp and started to cut the cakes in the darkness. Seokbong also began to write in the dark.

Finally, when he had finished writing, his mother relit the lamp. Seokbong was speechless when he saw that his mother had cut the rice cakes into perfectly even slices, whereas his writing was crooked and irregular. She scolded him vehemently, "Is this all you have to show for three years of study? Go back to

---

[3] In Korea, Buddhist temples often served as centers of education, as well as religious institutions.

the temple and study harder."

Seokbong wanted to stay with his mother for at least another day, but she would not allow it, and he was forced to leave home in the middle of the night. He walked away with tears falling from his eyes, but he knew that his mother's pain and sorrow were far greater than his own. After arriving at the temple, he kept his promise to his mother and studied even harder than before. Later, he became widely acknowledged as a calligrapher without equal, not only in Korea, but in neighboring countries as well.

* * * * *

The behavior of Han Seokbong's mother may appear strange at first. There is a Korean proverb which says, "Give one more stroke of the lash to a child you love." The meaning of the proverb is that if you really love a child and care about his future, you should be stern as well as kind, so that the child can correct his faults and become a better person. In the story, the mother's coldness was against her natural inclinations as a parent, but enabled her son to become more independent and devote himself more seriously to his studies. Another aspect of Eastern culture which can be seen from this story is the importance placed on education. A famous example is the story of the great Chinese scholar Mencius, whose mother is said to have moved house three times in order to find the best place for her son's education, finally choosing a house next door to a school.

Hong Chagi

In Chungju City of the Chungchong Province, there remains to this day a monument which Minister Yi Kahwan (1742~1801) built in memory of the dutiful son, Hong Chagi.

Chagi was born in Chungju in the 5th year of King Yongjo's reign (1759). Several months before his birth, Chagi's father had been falsely accused of murder and thrown into prison. Amidst these tragic circumstances, his mother Choi gave birth, and raised her son by herself.

When Chagi was ten years old, she told him the story of his father.

One day, after collecting firewood in the mountains, his father had stopped by at an inn for a drink, but left his axe behind. On the next day the innkeeper was found murdered with the same axe, and when Chagi's father returned that night to look for it, he was accused of the innkeeper's murder and arrested.

Chagi was astonished by his mother's story, and quickly made his way to the local government buildings in order to see his father. Upon seeing him in prison, Chagi bowed before him, and then burst into tears. Seeing his son for the first time in ten years, his father pressed himself against the cell door and wept with him. At this piteous sight, the prison guards were soon also in tears.

The young Chagi said, "Father, no matter what I must do, I will free you from these false charges and clear your name."

"Do not say that, child," his father said. "You are barely ten years old – how could you free me from prison? The only thing I ask of you is to forgive your bad father and serve your mother well. If the Heavens are merciful, the day will come when the three of us will embrace each other again."

On the following day, Chagi visited his senior relatives and asked them to put the unjust circumstances surrounding his father's conviction into writing. He then went to Seoul, and each day before the Royal Palace, held on to officials as they went past and showed them the papers, pleading with them to free his father. After twelve days, Chagi's story finally reached the ears of the King. The King therefore summoned the Minister of Justice, and having heard a full account, reduced the sentence on Chagi's father, and had him freed from prison and exiled to Yongnam.

Chagi was disappointed that his father had not obtained a full pardon. He followed his father in his exile and attended to him with great care, going back to Seoul whenever occasion allowed in order to bow before the Palace and plead his father's innocence.

Chagi's story gradually came to be known more widely among the officials, and the number of people who wished to help him grew. In the end, the King ordered the case to be re-opened. Chagi's father was found innocent in the investigation that followed, and released from exile.

In the meantime, Chagi, who had been running to and from Seoul day and night, collapsed from exhaustion. When he heard the news of his father's release, he was overjoyed, and offered up a prayer of gratitude to the Heavens. Before he could see his father return home, he passed away. He was then fourteen years old.

An Exchange of Bows

One day in the late spring, a provincial governor wished to go out and see the people of his province working in the rice paddies. It was near midday when the governor and his attendants set out, and all the farmers were having lunch.

The governor spent some time inspecting the rice fields, and then sat down to rest under a tree. From where he was sitting, he could see a lone farmer in the distance. A moment later, he saw a woman appear with a basket on her head. The farmer jumped up immediately and made towards the woman as if to scold her. It seemed that he was angry because she was late in bringing him his food.

The governor continued to watch the couple quietly. The wife appeared to spend some time explaining herself, and after a while, her husband suddenly put his hand on her arm and lowered his head.

The governor stood up, and was about to leave, when something strange happened. The couple suddenly began to bow to each other, not once but several times, again and again. Seeing this, the governor said to his attendants,

"How strange. Why have they started bowing to each other in the middle of an argument?"

"We should go and ask them," said one of his companions.

The governor and his attendants made their way to the farmer's field. Noticing that the governor was coming towards them, the couple quickly stood up in surprise and lowered their heads. The governor looked at them each in turn.

"Why were you bowing to each other just now?" he asked.

The farmer, trying to hold back his laughter, scratched his head, and said, "It was nothing."

"Speak," urged one of the attendants standing beside the governor.

Embarrassed, the farmer shuffled his feet and said,

"We rose at dawn to begin our work, and when lunchtime came, I sent my wife home to feed the baby and prepare some food for my aged mother. After that, I told her to bring some food for me. It was a long time before she brought me my lunch, and so I was full of anger when she arrived."

"But why did you bow to each other?" asked the governor.

"When my wife went home," the farmer explained, "she found my mother trying to catch a chicken because she wanted to eat chicken porridge, and saw that she had broken a jar of soy sauce by mistake. My wife quickly hid the broken jar so that my mother wouldn't feel bad, and then caught the chicken and made her chicken porridge. I was sorry for being angry before I knew the reason for her lateness, and grateful because she had cared for my mother so affectionately. And so I bowed to her, and she bowed back. But because I wanted her to receive a bow from me, I bowed again, and she also bowed again. So we ended up exchanging several bows."

After hearing this, the governor praised the couple for their filial devotion, and rewarded them.

The Boy Who Saved His Father's Life

In the reign of King Injo of the Choson Dynasty, there lived a man called Jo Chonsang, who lived in the county of Chongwon. His filial devotion was known even to the Royal Court.

One day, when Chonsang was in his tenth year, bandits from the mountains came to pillage his house. His father, who was a scholar and a poor man, hastily told the family to hide underneath the floor, while he himself attempted to fight off the intruders with a sword. However, as he was a scholar and not a soldier, he was no match for the bandits, and was soon captured and bound up with ropes.

The bandits began to search the house, and when they realized there was nothing to take, they threatened Chonsang's father, saying, "Where are the rest of your family? We don't need your belongings, just tell us where they are, and we will let you live."

The bandits were afraid that their faces would become known, and intended to kill them all.

"They have all gone to visit relatives. I am guarding the house by myself," the father replied.

"Don't lie! When we were coming here, we saw someone else with you. If you do not tell us the truth, we will set the house on fire."

The family listened in great apprehension, for the entire household was within an inch of being slaughtered.

"It is enough to kill just me, so why waste your time? Kill me now!"

"Do you think we will go just like that? Tell us!"

"Even if I knew, I would never tell you."

The bandits looked at one another. Venom flashed in their eyes, and among them a huge figure began to draw his sword. At the same time, the others prepared to depart. They had decided to kill Chonsang's father and leave.

The chief bandit raised his sword, his arm swelling with tension. His blade shimmered in the moonlight as the other bandits left one by one through the brushwood gate. The huge figure cast a sidelong glance at them, and then made to strike Chonsang's father with all his might.

In that very moment, a small figure ran beneath the sword. Startled, the bandit stepped back. Rolling on the ground with father in his arms was the young Jo Chonsang.

"Who are you?"

The bandit raised his sword once again.

"Don't kill my father!"

Chonsang shouted towards the bandit, shedding tears.

"Do you not have a father too? Kill me instead!"

Seeing the young Chonsang, the bandit could not bring himself to strike. He looked at the father and son in turn, then lowered his sword and fled.

Hyangdok's Devotion

In Kyongju City of ancient Silla, there lived a man named Hyangdok. He was gentle in nature and so faithful to his parents that talk of his virtue had spread to the neighboring villages.

In the 14th year of King Kyongdok's reign (755), there was a very poor harvest, and many people became ill for want of food. Hyangdok's mother developed a tumor, which grew worse as the days went on, until eventually her life was in danger.

Hyangdok nursed and tended his mother day and night, but was unable to obtain enough food for her to eat. Her body became thinner and her pain grew worse. He could not bear to see his mother's suffering.

Soon, the tumor spread to the bone, and as she could not endure the pain any longer, she began to cry and lament out loud. Hyangdok, unable to even look at her, said,

"If the tumor is not completely removed, your life will be at risk. I must suck out the pus."

His mother protested, but Hyangdok put his mouth to the tumor and sucked out the pus. A hole had formed in her skin where the tumor had begun, and a bowlful of pus flowed out.

Although Hyangdok sucked out a bowlful of pus every night, the tumor showed no signs of healing. Hyangdok found a doctor and asked him what medicine or treatment would cure the tumor. The doctor shook his head and told him, "If a tumor spreads to the bone, no medicine can cure it. If I were a great doctor, I might try to carve out the tumor from the bone, but her condition is so weak that even this may be impossible. However, if you keep feeding her nutritious food such as beef, she may eventually recover."

Unfortunately, Hyangdok could not afford to buy beef, and meat was in any case hard to come by in days of famine. Hyangdok returned home, and after sitting in deep thought for a while, went into the kitchen to get a knife, and started to cut out a piece of his thigh. The red blood streamed down his leg, but Hyangdok clenched his teeth and succeeded in carving out a lump of flesh.

That evening, he cooked it and served it to his mother. Her face lit up at the smell of the meat, and she asked him, "How did you get this? It must be extremely difficult to obtain meat these days."

"A neighbor of ours recently slaughtered a cow, and he gave me a small portion of it." Hyangdok replied.

His mother enjoyed the meat, unaware of the truth. From then on, little by little, her health recovered, and she was soon back on her feet. Hyangdok kept his wound hidden and lived just as he had before so that his mother would not notice anything. He dragged his crippled leg out to the field and worked hard, and occasionally went down to the river and caught fish to serve to his mother.

On one occasion, Hyangdok was out fishing, his leg still unhealed, and a provincial inspector who was passing by the river noticed a trace of blood in the water. Thinking it strange, he traveled further up the stream to investigate, and found a young man trying to catch a fish with blood dripping from his leg. He questioned him, and Hyangdok eventually told him the truth.

The inspector was so moved by his story that he reported it to the government. Word of it even reached the King, who praised Hyangdok greatly for his filial devotion, and rewarded him with 300 sacks of rice, a house, and some land on which to farm. The local government also erected a memorial and inscription in honor of Hyangdok and his devotion, which survives to this day.

A Strange Memorial Ceremony

A Royal inspector was once on his way to Kangwon Province. As evening began to draw in, the inspector decided to spend the night at a house on the road. When he entered the gates of the house he had chosen, he found the interior brightly lit with candles, and a group of people gathered in the courtyard.

"May I spend the night here?" he asked them.

A man who appeared to be the owner of the house came forward and said,

"I see no reason why not. As today we are holding a *chesa*[4] for our deceased father, please wait for a while in that room, and we will prepare a place for you to sleep after the ceremony is over."

The inspector waited in the room for a long time. When it seemed that the *chesa* had begun, he heard the people come out from the room where the ceremony was to be held, and saw the light from their lamps through the paper door. The inspector opened the door slightly and peered out. He saw the people leave the courtyard, and after vanishing into the darkness outside, they were gone for a long time. When they returned, he could hear them shouting.

"Father, here is a stream. Let us pass it by."

Even though there was no one to hear them, the family were talking continuously in this odd manner without a moment's pause. It was a very strange sight indeed.

---

[4] Memorial ceremony for ancestors. When a *chesa* is performed, Koreans believe that the spirits of their deceased ancestors come to their house and enjoy the food they prepare for them.

"Father, we are in front of the gate. Be careful not to trip up on the step."

"This is the yard. Mind that jagged rock."

"This is the patio. Take off your shoes."

"We have arrived. Please come and sit in front of the table."

The inspector looked very hard, but could not make out the person to whom they were speaking. He was overwhelmed with curiosity, but decided to wait until the *chesa* was over.

Soon after the ceremony had finished, the family went outside again. They proceeded just as they had done before the *chesa*, as if they were helping someone on their way.

"Did you enjoy the meal? Good bye then, and we will see you again at *Chusok* (Korean Thanksgiving)."

Later, the owner came with food and wine to the room where the inspector was waiting. The inspector asked, "You conduct your *chesa* ceremony very strangely. Why did the family go outside the house at the beginning and the end?"

Holding back a smile, the owner said, "The reason is that our father was blind. In the past, whenever he went out, we as his children always assisted him. So whenever we hold a *chesa*, in case he cannot find his way to our house, we go to his tomb to accompany him here, and then afterwards help him on his way."

The Inspector was deeply touched by their sincere affection for their blind father.

Pulguksa Temple

Built in the 8th century, UNESCO's World Cultural Heritage

Sim Chong

The Girl Who Became the Eyes of Her Father

One thousand years ago in Korea, in a village called Hwangju in Hwanghae Province, there lived a man named Sim Hakgyu. His family had in the past been well respected, and many of its members had served as public officials, but the family's wealth and reputation had over time declined. As one misfortune tends to ride upon another's back, Sim contracted a severe disease when he was a teenager, and although he survived, was left blind as a result. Becoming blind at such an early age, he had no hope of becoming a public official, which was at the time the only respectable occupation for those of noble birth. From then on, the town folk called him Blind Sim.

Sim had a gentle disposition, and lived his life decently and modestly. At the age of 20, he married a woman from the Kwak family. She was also of good conduct, and very wise and beautiful. Because they were very poor, the kind-hearted Lady Kwak was obliged to perform needlework and other menial tasks in order to support herself and her husband, while attending to him with great love and care. Although their possessions were few, the love and affection they had for each other were the envy of everyone.

Sim, however, was often heard to sigh deeply. One day, he said to his wife, "There are many married couples in the world. But there is no wife like you, who work so hard and so well to support and take care of me, as if you were tending to a young child. While I am as comfortable as I can be because of your efforts, my mind is not at ease because of the great hardships that you have to bear. There is no need to have such concern for me, since I am happy with us living as we are. There is, however, one thing we lack. Even though we are in our forties, we have no child to perform the *chesa* for us when we are gone. How will we face our ancestors in heaven, if we do not have a child to perform ceremonies for them too? When we die, who will be there to arrange the funeral, and who will prepare food, a bowl of rice, or even a cup of water, for our *chesa*?"

The Lady Kwak answered gently, "According to the scriptures, there are three thousand offenses that one can commit against one's parents, and not bringing forth a child is the gravest of all. I have also sincerely wished for a child, but I did not say anything because we are poor and because I did not know your feelings. Now that I do, I will pray for a child with all my heart."

It was already difficult for her to meet the expenses of the household by herself, but she saved what little money she could from her work, and visited many famous mountains and temples to make offerings and to pray for a child.

After three years had gone by since she began her offerings and prayers, she had a dream on the night of the Buddha's birthday. In the dream, an angel from heaven, riding on the back of a crane, flew into her bosom and said, "I am sent by Buddha. Please receive me." She woke up, greatly surprised by the dream. When she told Sim about it, she was amazed to hear that her husband had had exactly the same dream. Excited and full of joy, he said, "Surely, this dream foretells your giving birth. Buddha must have been moved by your earnest prayers, and so he has sent us a child."

Three or four months later, Lady Kwak began to show signs of pregnancy, and after ten months she gave birth to a daughter. As Sim tenderly caressed the baby, he thanked his wife, "You have endured much hardship. Do people not say that daughters are the root of a family's fortune? Let us raise our daughter to be a great person, so that we need never be envious of another's son."

However, their time of joy was soon cut short. After giving birth, Lady

Kwak fell ill. Sim sent for a doctor in the neighboring village, but medicine seemed to do her no good, and her condition worsened daily.

One day, she called her husband to her, saying she had one final wish.

"I don't think that I can live much longer. But the thought of leaving you and the baby behind fills my heart with grief."

"Oh, my dear wife," Sim said, "Do not be so weak. How can I leave without you?"

Lady Kwak said, "When I think of you begging for food from door to door with blind eyes and only a cane to guide your uncertain steps, and of my daughter who will never taste her mother's milk, and will be scorned for being motherless, tears block my eyes, and I cannot see the path that leads to the nether world. If, by chance, our baby survives and with the help of the heaven grows up to walk on her own feet, please have her lead you to my tomb and tell her that it is where her mother lies. Then, at least, I will have no regrets in death. Since I can do nothing but follow the will of the Heavens, who are now taking back my life, I must go before you. Do not let your health suffer because of grief, my dear. Let us meet again in our next life, and continue in our love for each other, never to be parted. As for the child, please name her Chong. "

"Chong?"

"Yes, it means eyes. And my hope is that she will become your eyes in helping you."

"As you wish."

"Chong," the lady Kwak lamented with her final breaths, "the heavens are merciless! As my death comes at your birth, I leave you beneath an unbearable sorrow. Who will feed you? In whose bosom will you sleep at night?"

The tears ran down her face in streams. Before long, the sound of her breathing could not be heard, and her body grew cold. When Sim realized that his wife was dead, he struck his chest and beat his head against the wall in sorrow.

"My dear, if you had lived and I had died, you would have been able to raise the child. But instead, I am alive and you are dead. How am I to raise her by myself? How am I to survive in this wretched state? And if I take my own life, what will become of the baby? No, my dear, do not die. Do not die…"

Hearing the news of Lady Kwak's death, the people of the village kindly offered to take care of her funeral. Sim, when he returned from the ceremony, found his house lonelier than ever before. He wandered here and there, overwhelmed with grief and sorrow, and even called out for his wife. When he heard the sound of the baby crying, he brought a bowl of water from the kitchen. After dipping his finger in the water, he put it to the baby's mouth. At first, she sucked on his finger thinking the water was her mother's milk. But when it did not satisfy her hunger, she began to cry again. All night long, Sim tried to soothe the baby until he heard the rooster crowing at dawn.

Not having slept, with a disheveled appearance, he left his house and followed the path outside it, always dark and perilous for him, holding the child in one arm and a cane in his hand. Somehow, he had to feed the baby. First, he went to the mother of Kwidok, a friend of his wife. He called out to her, "Dear lady, please spare some milk for poor motherless Chong."

Kwidok's mother said, "Please come in right away. How pitiful that this little baby has lost her mother and must grow up in the care of her blind father."

She breastfed Chong and prepared breakfast for Sim. She then went from door to door looking for mothers with babies, saying "Let us spare some milk for Sim's daughter."

Others replied, "We cannot ignore the condition of our poor neighbor. We will feed her and also provide meals for Sim." So, out of sympathy, everyone tried to help the poor man. Every morning, Sim went out searching for someone to feed Chong, calling out to the women washing clothes or working in the field.

Although she was raised on food obtained from begging, Chong grew up healthily, never once falling ill with the common diseases. She became a beautiful girl who performed her duties to her father conscientiously. She prepared meals for her father every day and even learned to hold the *chesa* ceremony for her mother.

Once she was able to walk, she accompanied her father to beg for food. She would lead the way, holding on to the cane, while Sim held the other end, making it much easier for him to walk.

When she turned six, Chong said, "Father, I am always anxious about you, fearing that you may fall from a high place or into a deep pit. Also, if the weather becomes cold because of rain and snow, I am afraid that you may become ill. From now on, please stay at home and let me beg for food on your behalf."

Sim answered, "That is very kind of you, but do you think I can let you go and beg for food, when you are still only a child? Do not speak of this again, my dear." Chong, however, pleaded with her father until in the end he had to agree.

When she went to beg for food by herself, the villagers were even more generous to her and her father. Out of sympathy, they often said, "Why don't you stay and join us for a meal?" She would always politely reply, "You are very kind. But how can I eat here by myself when my old father is waiting for me in a cold house? I should hurry back home and eat with him."

When Sim heard Chong's returning footsteps, he would open the door wide and welcome her in. He would blow on her frozen hands and rub her feet to warm them. Then, he would say to her, "Because of my blindness, you suffer such hardships in this freezing weather." The devoted Chong comforted her father by saying, "Father, please do not talk this way. It is the duty of children to take care of their parents, and to be cared for by one's child is a parent's natural right."

As she grew older, Chong's skill in needlework became equal to that of her late mother. Since she could earn a living by needlework, she no longer had to beg for food. She was now able to pay for her father's clothes and food with what she earned from her work.

When she was sixteen, Chong was sent for by a widowed noblewoman who lived in the neighboring village, whose late husband had been Prime Minister. Although Chong's clothes were ragged, the lady was impressed by Chong's untainted appearance and modest demeanor.

"Both of my sons are in Seoul serving the King as officials," she said to Chong, "and I have become lonely living by myself in this big house. I would like to adopt you as my daughter. Would you like that?"

Chong replied, "After my mother passed away within seven days of my birth, my blind father raised me by begging for milk. Since you have kindly asked me to become your daughter, I am as pleased and honored as if I had met my own mother. But if I were to accept, who would take care of my blind father, without whom I could not have survived until now? Therefore, although there is very little I can do for my father, I prefer to stay with him."

The lady was touched by Chong's devotion to her father. She asked Chong not to forget her and to always think of her as her mother nonetheless. Meanwhile, Sim was worrying about Chong, because it was very late and she had not yet returned. He was so anxious that he was no longer able to sit and wait for her. He decided to go out to look for her himself, with only his cane to assist him. Because it had been a long while since he had been outside by himself, it was very difficult for him to walk. As he was making his way across a creek, he slipped and fell into waters almost two meters deep. His face turned dark with shock, and his wet clothes began to freeze. No one answered his cry for help, and he could hear only the sound of the cold wind blowing.

"It seems that I will die far away from home in this freezing water," he lamented.

When he had almost given up hope, a monk from Mong-un temple heard his screaming and came to pull him out.

"Who is that? Who has saved my wretched life?" Sim asked.

The monk replied, "I am a monk from Mong-un temple."

Feeling pity for Sim, the monk said quietly to himself, "If he could only offer up 300 sacks of rice to Buddha, he would regain his sight."

When Sim heard this, he almost doubted his ears.

"What? Can I regain my sight if I offer up rice to Buddha?"

The monk answered, "Yes, of course. As Buddha's follower, I would not speak vainly of such things."

Sim felt more miserable about himself than ever before. Thinking only of regaining his sight, he vowed to offer up 300 sacks of rice to the Buddha, and signed his name "Sim Hakgyu" in the monk's book.

"You must keep your promise to Buddha," the monk warned, "or you will receive severe retribution." He then went on his way.

Arriving back home, completely soaked, Sim began to regret what he had done. It was reckless of him to have made such a promise when he knew that he had barely enough money to keep himself alive. He was seized with remorse for his stupidity. At the same time, he was very afraid at the thought of the punishment that he would receive for not fulfilling his promise.

Chong came home and was surprised to see her father soaking wet and full of anxious thoughts. She asked him the reason, but Sim kept silent and would not say anything. Chong prepared supper for him with the food that she received from the household of the noblewoman. Sim, however, seemed to have lost his appetite.

Chong asked him, "Father, you have always trusted me, as I have trusted you. We have discussed all manner of things together in the past. What is wrong today?"

When she continued to question him, Sim finally relented and told her everything – how he had fallen, how the monk had saved his life, and how he had promised to offer up 300 sacks of rice to the Buddha.

Chong said, "Father, do not worry. If it is possible for you to regain your sight, we should leave nothing untried." Rather than scolding him, kind-hearted Chong tried to comfort her father.

But she was also worried about her father's promise. Each night, she went outside with a bowl of pure water as her offering, and prayed, "Lord Buddha, please give my father back his sight. I will offer myself to you if it will restore sight to my father's eyes."

Ten days after she began her prayers, Chong overheard her neighbors having a conversation.

"Have you heard? Some sailors are trying to buy a 16-year-old girl to offer as a sacrifice." Hearing this, Chong found the sailors and asked them, "Why do you need to buy a girl?"

"We are merchants who are sailing to China. In order to go to China, we have to pass a region called Indangsu, which is fraught with dangerous currents and thick fogs, and shipwrecks frequently happen there. Every few years, for the safety of our ships, we make an offering of a maiden at Indangsu in order to appease the ocean. This is the year in which we have to make such an offering."

Chong said, "In that case, please buy me."

When she had explained her desperate situation, the sailors agreed to give 300 sacks of rice, moved by her piety.

"We will come back for you when the moon is full."

Chong asked them to send the rice to the Mongun temple, without her father knowing.

Chong was delighted that her father could keep his promise to Buddha and that he could now regain his sight. Although she would die, she felt that there was nothing more important than this.

"Father," she said, "We can now offer up 300 sacks of rice to the Mongun temple."

Sim was taken aback, "What? How? What are you saying? Are you mocking your father?"

Chong said, "No, father. I would not dare."

"Then how did you obtain so much rice?"

"A few days ago, when I went to visit a noble lady, she asked me to become her adopted daughter."

Sim asked, "Why did she want to make you her adopted daughter?"

Chong replied, "She must have taken a liking to me. She found out about our situation and offered to give 300 sacks of rice."

"How very kind of her!"

Sim believed Chong and was overjoyed.

"Does that mean you must go and live with her now?"

"Yes, I agreed to join her when the moon is full. But I am worried about you, since you will have to live by yourself."

"Don't worry about me. It is good that you can now lead a comfortable life. As for me, since I will regain my sight, there are many things that I can do to support myself."

Chong was in tears as she witnessed her father's happiness. She thought to herself, "When he finds out later that I have been sacrificed as an offering, he will be mortified."

Her heart was heavy with sorrow, but she could not give in to her grief, as she had to prepare for her departure. She washed all her father's clothes and put them neatly in his cupboard so that he could easily find them. She also dusted off her father's old hat. She pulled up the weeds in the garden and swept every corner of the house. The day before her departure, she visited her mother's grave, and wept pitifully as she said farewell.

"Mother, this will be my last visit to you. Please look after my poor father."

At home, also, she sobbed silently at her father's bedside.

"My dear father, please forgive the lies of your unworthy daughter. Open your eyes wide and live happily."

When dawn approached, Chong's eyes were swollen from crying all night long.

At breakfast, her father said, "Chong, our food today tastes more delicious than usual. Is this not the day when you are to move to the noblewoman's household? In my dream last night, I saw you traveling far away in a beautiful carriage. This dream surely foretells that you are going to a wonderful place." Sim then told Chong to get herself ready.

Hearing her father say these things in ignorance of what was going to happen, Chong could no longer hold back her tears.

"My poor father!" she cried, "How can I leave you by yourself?"

"Chong, do not cry. We will be able to see each other again."

Chong could no longer deceive her father. She confessed that she had sold herself for 300 sacks of rice.

"Chong, what do you mean? If you die, what use is my sight? Although blind, I have been able to live untroubled ever since your mother passed away, for you have been my eyes. If I kill my child to gain sight and happiness, it would not be true joy. Can deceiving your father be filial devotion? I do not want to gain my sight and I am not afraid of breaking my promise to Buddha. Go now, and tell them that the promise is void."

The villagers heard Sim shouting these words, and gathered around Sim's house. When the neighbors heard the sad tale, they all shed tears in sympathy. Sim begged his daughter not to go, holding on to the sleeves of her robes, but Chong said, "In breaking your vow to Buddha, you will bring a great calamity upon yourself. Breaking my promise to the sailors would not be right either. So, father, please let me go. How could I dare to dishonor the obligation of a daughter to her father, which is ordained by nature? In doing this, I am only following the will of Heaven."

Then she tore herself away and, wiping the tears from her eyes, bowed down to her father. The villagers held on to Sim to restrain him, and Chong ran from the house.

"Chong!" her father cried, "My poor child! Please do not leave! Stay here, and I will go in your place." Chong felt her father's wailing pierce her heart, and covered her ears as she followed the sailors. The clear sky suddenly turned dark and began to scatter rain, as if sharing their sorrow.

The ship carrying Chong made its way swiftly across the ocean. Suddenly, an enormous wave was seen coming towards the ship with such force and speed that it looked as if it would engulf it entirely.

"This is Indangsu!" the sailors cried. "Make ready!"

Chong changed into new robes, and kneeled down. Folding her hands, she began to pray to Buddha.

"Buddha, receive my prayer. Please take me and give my father back his sight, so that he can look upon this beautiful world."

She prayed again, and asked a favor of the sailors.

"I wish you a safe journey and a prosperous outcome. Please go and see my father when you return. Find out if he has regained his sight, and if he is living well."

"Have no concern about that. May you go to a better place, sweet maiden."

The sailors began to beat their drums. Chong climbed up to the prow. She looked up to the sky, towards her home and her father. Then she closed her eyes and threw herself into the raging sea.

Having received an offering of a beautiful flower, the ocean gradually became calm. The sailors all said, "It is clearly this girl, with her deep filial devotion, that has calmed the waves."

The Great Hyo of Emperor Shun

The Emperors Yao and Shun of ancient China were wise and noble rulers, who blessed their nation with peace and lasting prosperity.

When Emperor Yao approached old age, he began to look for a successor. He gave an order to his courtiers to find him "the greatest example of filial piety." His courtiers unanimously recommended Dan Zhu, one of his nine sons, as his successor. The Emperor replied, "My son Dan Zhu is unworthy to be ruler of China." He instructed them to search more widely for a person of great filial devotion, for he considered this to be the greatest virtue that a ruler should possess.

After receiving the Emperor's order, the courtiers traveled the length and breadth of the land hoping to discover a suitable candidate. Since they were unable to find anyone within China, they crossed the border into Korea. In the end, a farmer who lived in a village called Harbin, on the eastern side of the Liao River, was chosen. He has been known to posterity as Emperor Shun.

In the Confucian Canon of Li Lau, Mencius notes, "Since Shun was born in Chû-fang, moved to Fû-hsiâ, and died in Ming-t'iâo, he is a man from Tong-yi (Korea)." Before he became Emperor, Shun lived by plowing the fields, planting crops, making pottery and catching fish.

He lost his mother at an early age and was raised by his stepmother, a spiteful woman who treated him with great cruelty, and regarded him as a thorn in her side. One day, she told him to dig a hole in the ground. Her plan was to wait until the hole was deep enough, and then to bury her stepson alive.

Because of his sense of duty, Shun could not disobey his stepmother's words, although he was aware of her plan. He simply replied "Yes" and began to dig the hole as he had been told. But he was not buried alive, for as he dug the hole he was to be buried in, he also dug another hole through which he could come out.

On another day, Shun's stepmother ordered him to climb the roof so that he could mend a leak in it. After Shun had climbed up, she removed the ladder and set fire to the house. Once again, however, Shun survived. For being aware of his stepmother's intention, he took a second ladder with him and used it to climb down.

Even when subjected to such treatment from his stepmother, Shun never harbored resentment against his parents, but simply pleaded to the Heavens with tears. He knew that the Rose of Althea was a flower that bloomed in the morning and wilted in the evening, and so he planted it in the garden of his house. Looking upon it day and night, he would reflect that just as the bloom of the flower did not last long, the time when he could serve his parents would also be short.

In the end, his utmost devotion moved his parents, and because of his great *hyo*, he rose to the throne of the Emperor.

The Virtue of Hyo

There are numerous kinds of virtuous deeds; the root of all is filial piety.
There are numerous kinds of sinful deeds; the root of all is filial impiety.

- Korean maxim -

The virtue of *Hyo*, or filial devotion, has a long history in Korea, and was traditionally considered to be the foremost measure of person's character and worth. Koreans throughout the ages have believed that since our parents brought us into this world and raised us, being grateful to them and serving them well is the most basic of all human virtues.

Among the East Asian countries that have been influenced by Confucianism, Korea is the country where filial devotion is most deeply rooted and where the tradition remains strongest. Because the root of Japanese culture is in the *Samurai*, loyalty to the king was traditionally given greater emphasis than loyalty to one's parents. A word such as *hyoja*, for example, which means "devoted son" in Korean, does not exist in Japanese. Whereas a Korean woman will never change her last name, which her parents gave to her, in Japan a woman always takes her husband's last name, as the duty of a wife to her husband is held to be more important than filial duty.

In China, there is also a strong tradition of *Hyo*, although not as pronounced as that of Korea. China's renowned sage Confucius so greatly admired and respected the Korean Emperor Shun that he referred to him as "The Great Hyo".

Confucius said, "Shun is 'The Great Hyo.' His virtue was that of a sage, his nobility that of an emperor, and his wealth encompassed the whole world. He offered ceremonies to the ancestors, and preserved the integrity of his descendents."

– The Doctrine of the Mean (中庸)

Mencius praised Shun's filial piety in the following passage:

Men, when they are young, have strong attachments to their parents. When they come to learn of the carnal pleasures, they yearn for young and beautiful women. When they have a family, they have a strong attachment to that family. When they obtain a position in the government, they revere the monarch. However, if they are not able to obtain the confidence of the monarch, they develop a febrile disease in the chest. The "Great Hyo" served his parents throughout his entire life, until the age of 50 [the age where Shun left his home and rose to the emperor's throne in China].

– Commentary on Mencius (孟子集註)

This tradition of filial piety made Korea a pleasant and civilized country. Confucius himself stated that, "the well-mannered monarchy in the east" was the place where he himself would like to live.

According to Korean custom, one should be humble before others, and speak and behave in a respectful manner to one's parents. Koreans use different words according to the level of respect owed to the person addressed. A parent's birthday, for example, was called *saeng-sin*, an older sibling's birthday *saeng-il*, and one's own birthday *dol*.

When Koreans refer to themselves in front of their parents, they use the word "jeo" or "je" – the humble word for "I." When conversing with parents, they use formal sentences ending in "sub-ni-da." Among all the peoples in the world, Koreans are the only people who have such strict and detailed honorific expressions. The Korean word "jeo" or "je" could be translated into similarly humble expressions of "I" such as "小子", "小生" or "卑生" in Chinese, but there is no equivalent of "sub-ni-da." In Japanese, where there is an equivalent of "sub-ni-da" although it is not as distinct as in Korean, words such as "watakusi" or "boku" meaning "I" do exist, but they are not used to lower oneself like the Korean "jeo" or "je". The Korean words and expressions that allow people to lower themselves developed from the language used in the home.

As well as speaking respectfully, bowing is an important part of the decorum of filial devotion. Children express their respect for their parents by lowering their head, which is the most important part of the body, to the floor. According to custom, when a devoted son or daughter was traveling to distant place, they would bow in front of their parents before departing for the journey, and again upon their return.

Traditionally in Korea, children did not allow their parents to live by themselves when they became old. Instead, they supported them with good food and clothes until the end of their lives. Even when the parents passed away due to old age, the children believed that they were somehow responsible for their parents' death. Those who had lost their father or mother would build a hut next to their parent's grave and live there for three years, paying respects to the deceased twice a day. The tradition was called *simyo,* which literally means "serving at a parent's grave," and was an expression of gratitude on the part of the bereaved to the parent who had taken care of them for the first three years of their lives, when they could not have survived without their help. Even today, some people follow this tradition.

Until the 1950s, there were many Koreans who performed daily memorial services for their parents for a period of one to three years after they had died. Every morning, they would prepare breakfast for their mother and father, and bow down to the shrine of the deceased. Only after this had been done would the rest of the family have breakfast. Because Koreans believed that they were obliged to repay the debt they owed to their deceased parents by performing such services, they carried them out with the greatest care. While this tradition is not practiced to the same extent nowadays, many Korean families still perform such memorial services at least three times a year, on New Year's day, the festival of Autumn Moon (August 15th in lunar calendar), and the date on which their parents passed away. On performing the memorial service, respects are paid not only to parents, but also to ancestors, going back three, sometimes as many as five, generations. Without our parents, we could not have existed, nor could our parents have existed without our grandparents, and so on. It thanks to our ancestors that we are here today.

These days, men and women usually prefer to choose their own spouses, but until as recently as three decades ago, Koreans trusted their parents to choose partners for them, and families were begun in this way. Newly-wedded wives would go to live with their husband's family and learn about their customs and etiquette. The married couple would attend to their elders with care and deference. They would visit their parents' room every morning and evening to pay their respects, and would begin to eat only after the elder family members had begun their meals.

Hyo is the act of repaying the love and grace of another person. Koreans believed that the love of their parents was as precious as the grace of the Heavens. Thus, they lived their lives by repaying that love with gratitude and devotion to their parents. Filial devotion to parents is learned by children, and handed down by them to their own children.

Gratitude and respect for one's parents is the root of the greater love and understanding that embraces the whole of humanity – since everyone is the parent or child of someone else.

Wolgwangmun (Gate of Moonlight) of Changdok Palace

Chapter 2

Chung: Loyalty to Country and People

Ulpaso

Able ministers play an important role during a period of reform in any government or dynasty. When King Kogukchon (r. 179~197 AD) of Koguryo oversaw a series of reforms in his own government, he had a wise prime minister called Ulpaso, who would long be remembered in history for his great intelligence and compassion.

During the Koguryo Dynasty (BC 37~AD 668), which began as a confederacy of five tribes, it was the custom to select a member from the royal family of each tribe to serve as a government minister, so that each tribe would have a share in the rule of the country. King Kogukchon, however, broke with this tradition and began to select officials on the basis of merit. As a result of this measure, the standard of Kokuryo's government improved.

"Until this time," the King declared, "positions in the government have been given on grounds of family and social status. The highest posts in the government should be granted to those of ability and virtue. By not following this practice, we have done harm to both the Royal Court and the people's interests. From this day forward, I will appoint only officials who possess the necessary virtues and abilities for their position. Therefore, let a wise person be chosen from each clan and nominated before the country."

Through this process, a man named Anryu was chosen. However, he declined the role, and in his own place put forward a man named Ulpaso.

"Ulpaso? Who is he?" the court murmured.

"He is a descendant of Ulso," Anryu said, "who served as a government minister during the reign of King Yurimyong. He is a man of upright character and great intelligence, and is knowledgeable in the affairs of the world. He is not a man of great fortune, and currently lives as a farmer in a remote village. If your highness wishes to rule the country well, let him be brought before the royal court."

The King had Ulpaso summoned into the court's presence. Despite his rustic appearance, the King saw from his eyes that he was a man of refinement.

The King said, "If I appoint you as a government minister, will you work diligently on your country's behalf?"

Ulpaso shook his head from side to side.

"Because I am very stupid," he replied, "I am not qualified to carry out your highness' command. I request, therefore, that your highness choose a wiser person, appoint him to a high position, and entrust him with the duty of serving the country."

The meaning behind these words was that Ulpaso intended to serve the country well in any case, and so the King should bestow upon him the highest rank, thus allowing him to serve it to the fullest extent. King Kogukchon immediately understood the meaning of Ulpaso's words and appointed him as Prime Minister so that he would have the power to do as he wished. However, this caused much consternation in the King's court. Ulpaso attracted much criticism from the courtiers, who were jealous that a poor, lowly man from the countryside should rise to the highest position in the King's government overnight.

Due to the widespread complaints regarding Ulpaso's appointment, the King made the following proclamation, "If any official defies the Prime Minister's command, he and his family will be put to death." With this decree, the King showed even greater confidence in Ulpaso. Deeply moved by the fact that he had met a ruler who recognized his abilities, Ulpaso wholeheartedly devoted himself to governing the country, delivered fair judgments, and issued wise orders and decrees.

One day, Ulpaso approached the King and said,

"Your highness, the purpose of the government is to serve the people. Therefore, it is only when the King and his ministers are concerned with the sufferings of the people that the people will love their country and follow their King like a father. Every year, in early spring, people go hungry because of the scarcity of food, and there are many who starve to death."

"I know this well," the King replied, "however, there seems to be nothing that we can do to solve this problem. What is your opinion?"

"I was considering, your highness, that we might establish a system whereby the grain in the state reserves might be lent to those who have none set aside, until they were able to pay it back. When food becomes difficult to obtain in March, the granaries could be opened up to those in need. Then in October, after the harvest is over, people could give back grain and return what they had borrowed."

King Kogukchon was astonished and replied,

"This is surely wisdom sent from the Heavens. It is your great care for the people that has enabled you to conceive of this. Now, see that it is carried out in the best way possible."

This was the origin of the government loan called *Chindaebop*. At the time the decree was passed, almost two millennia ago, it was an almost revolutionary measure. The practice of allowing people to borrow grain from the state, so that they could avoid starvation, continued during the subsequent Koryo (918~1392) and Choson (1392~1910) dynasties, bearing witness to the wisdom of Ulpaso.

Without the people, there can be no country. Ulpaso, who established the fundamental rule that a country is responsible for the well-being of its people, is rightly remembered as one of the greatest prime ministers in Korean history.

The Loyal Spirit of Pak Chesang

When Naemul, the 17th King of Silla, passed away, his eldest son, Nulji, was too young to take the throne. Therefore Naemul's nephew, Silsong, was chosen to be the 18th King of Silla.

In the first year of King Silsong's reign (402), Japan dispatched an envoy to Silla proposing friendship, requesting that a Royal Prince be sent to them as a sign of trust. King Silsong did not refuse, and sent the third son of King Naemul, Prince Misahun, to visit the Royal Court of Japan. As the prince was only ten years old, one of his courtiers accompanied him as deputy-ambassador. When Prince Misahun and the courtier arrived, the Japanese King held them as political hostages and refused to let them return.

Ten years later, in the year 412, the neighboring kingdom of Koguryo sent an envoy to Silla to obtain an agreement of friendship.

"Having learned of the distinguished wisdom and abilities of the Prince Pokho, the King of Koguryo wishes to make his acquaintance, and hereby sends us to make this request."

King Silsong was at the time looking for a way to make peace with Koguryo, whose troops were carrying out many raids on the borders of Silla. He therefore replied expressing his wish for peace, and bid the second son of King Naemul, Prince Pokho, leave for Koguryo to bear this message for him. However, when he arrived, King Kwanggaeto of Koguryo detained Prince Pokho at his court and refused to let him go.

With the passing of time, the young Nulji grew up, and eventually became the 19th King of Silla in 417. King Nulji's mind, however, was constantly troubled with the thought of his two younger brothers. But although he longed to bring them back, there was little he could do.

One day, the King invited royal courtiers, celebrated scholars and military officials to the Palace in order to give them a banquet. When the wine bowl had gone round three or four times and the banquet was almost at its height, the King was unable to hold back his sorrow, and burst into tears, saying,

"My two younger brothers are prisoners in Japan and Koguryo, and are to this day unable to return to their homeland. Although I have come to this position of wealth and honor, not a day goes by without my thinking of them, not a day when I am not in mourning. Our ties as brothers drive the pain of absence deeper into my heart. If I could meet my two brothers again and go with them to the tomb of our late king to offer my apologies, in my gratitude I would reward everyone present at this feast. I must see to it that they return alive, but how am I to do so?"

The courtiers replied,

"Your Majesty, since this is no easy task, only one equipped with both wisdom and courage will be able to succeed in it. The governor of Sapra, Pak Chesang, as we have heard, is honorable, courageous, wise and resourceful. We are certain that he can relieve your Majesty of this burden."

Pak Chesang was a descendant of Pak Hyokgose, the founder of the Silla dynasty, and a 5th generation descendant of King Pasa, the fifth sovereign of Silla. He had served as a courtier since the time of King Naemul.

King Nulji summoned Pak Chesang to the Court, and entreated him to rescue the two Princes. To this, Pak replied,

"It is written, your Majesty, that if the King is troubled, his courtiers are thereby dishonored, and if the King is dishonored, his courtiers must die for it. If I were to go forward in this task discriminating the easy from the difficult, that would not be true loyalty, and if I hesitated, fearing death, that would not be courage. Though your servant is foolish and unworthy, how could he consider any other course than to serve and uphold your Majesty's wish?" With these words, Pak Chesang began to make the necessary preparations for an embassy, and set out for Koguryo.

When he was in the presence of the King of Koguryo, he earnestly entreated him,

"Your Majesty, it is well remarked that relationships between upright nations should be governed by faithfulness above all else. If we must exchange political hostages, a practice unheard of even during the days of the Five Tyrants[5], we are indeed living in desperate times. It has been nearly ten years since the younger brother of our King arrived in this country. Because of the ties of brotherly love that exist between these two men, neither can forget the other. As befits the ruler of a vast nation, show mercy and benevolence. If by the grace of your Imperial Majesty, Prince Pokho returns to Silla, your loss will be no greater than that of one hair from the hides of nine bulls, and our King's respect for your virtue will be boundless. Please reflect on this in your heart, your Majesty."

Moved by his words, the King of Koguryo agreed to his request, and bade him and the prince return together.

When Pak Chesang came back with Prince Pokho, King Nulji was overjoyed. But after some time had passed, he said, "I used to consider my two younger brothers as my right and left arm. Now that I have only regained one, what shall I do about the other?"

Pak Chesang replied,

"Though your servant lacks wisdom and is a man of little account, he has

---

[5] Mencius said, "To disguise power as benevolence is tyranny, to practice benevolence with virtue is kingship." This was a direct criticism of the rulers of his day, whose quest for power Mencius likened to those of the "Five Tyrants," which included Huan Gong of the Liang Kingdom. Mencius' Five Tyrants have since been used as a term of censure against despotic regimes in Far Eastern Asia.

already resolved to sacrifice himself for his country, and will not allow your Majesty's reign to labor any more under this disgrace. For what reason should I spare my life? As Koguryo is a great Kingdom, and its king is virtuous, I was able to persuade him with words and entreaties. In the case of Japan, however, since they are lacking in righteousness, they cannot be appeased by mere words, and we can only hope to rescue the prince by cunning. Therefore, your Highness, when I leave for Japan, see to it that my name is brought into disrepute, and spread rumors to make it appear that I have left the country in anger, so that the Japanese may hear them and believe."

Saying this, Pak pledged to offer his life. Without even visiting his home, he made his way to Yulpo, and immediately set sail for Japan.

When Pak's wife, who had been anxiously awaiting her husband's return, heard that he had gone directly to Yulpo from the Palace, she hurried to the port herself. When she arrived, the ship that her husband had boarded was already far out to sea. Seeing the ship in the distance, she wailed bitterly and called out.

"Please come back safely!"

Pak replied to her, "Entrusted by Royal Order with a task of great difficulty, I am sailing to the country of our enemies. I can therefore give no thought to my return. Please do not wait for me, my wife." With these words, he sailed onwards. Collapsing on the shore, Pak's wife wept and wept. The villagers later named the shore *Jang Sa,* which means "the shore of many tears."

When Pak arrived in Japan, on the pretence that he had betrayed Silla, he convinced the Japanese King that he had severed ties with his homeland.

"Though I gave my utmost loyalty to King Nulji of Silla, I received nothing in return but humiliation and disgrace. When I came back from Koguryo as the royal envoy, he accused me of treason and tried to have me executed. I no longer wish to serve a man such as Nulji, who cannot recognize true loyalty in those who attend him. I pray, your Imperial Highness, that you will show mercy and receive me as your humble servant."

The Japanese king had heard from a spy he had previously sent to Silla that Governor Pak's family had been imprisoned on charges of treason, and so he believed his words. It also occurred to him that Pak Chesang might be of use when he next invaded Silla.

Pak's considerable talents and character ensured that he soon joined the King's circle of trusted courtiers, and was able to approach Prince Misahun at will. Although Pak would sometimes go fishing or hunting with the Prince, he never acted in a way that would raise suspicion.

In the fall of 418, the Japanese King attempted an invasion of Silla, breaking his promises of peace. Appointing Pak and Misahun as his generals, he made them lead the way.

Arriving at Tsushima Island, which lies halfway between Silla and Japan, several of the Japanese generals gathered together, and began to lay plans in secret to capture and bring back the wives and children of Pak and Misahun once they had defeated Silla, thinking that this way they could be certain of their loyalty. Pak was aware of what they were doing, and pretended to amuse himself catching fish on the boat with Misahun. The Japanese, noting this, were pleased to see that the two had no secret plans of their own.

At dawn on the next day, when the fog had spread thickly, Pak Chesang urged Prince Misahun to flee. "Today is ideal for your escape. Please, go with all speed."

Misahun replied, "How could I leave you and return alone, when I have followed and depended on you like a father? I will not go."

Pak said, "If we both go, it is likely that we will fail. When I left Silla, I had already resolved to die. Please go, and do not concern yourself about me."

Upon hearing these words, Misahun embraced him and wept. He bid him farewell, and then began to make his way to Silla. Seeing him leave, Park returned to his room and rose late on the next day, pretending that he was exhausted, so as to give Misahun more time to make his escape.

Several men asked him, "General, why have you risen so late?" Pak replied, "Traveling by ship yesterday made me very tired, and I was unable to rise earlier." When people inquired as to why they had not seen the Prince that day, he explained that the Prince was also tired from yesterday's fishing and was still resting in his room. When Misahun did not appear even after sunset, however, the Japanese became suspicious, and discovered that he had escaped. They imprisoned Pak and immediately gave chase with their ships. But as the fog was thick and the sky was already dark, they could not see very far, and were in the end unable to catch Misahun.

"Why did you send him back?" the Japanese King asked him, seething with rage.

"I am a servant of Silla," Park calmly replied, "not a servant of Japan. I have done no more than carry out the will of my King. What other explanation need I offer?"

The Japanese King replied,

"You say that you serve Silla, when you are even now my servant? If you persist in saying this, I will subject you to the Five Torments. If you admit that you are a vassal of Japan, you will receive my full forgiveness."

Because the Japanese King esteemed Pak's courage and wisdom very highly, he promised that if he became his courtier, he would not only forgive him and spare his life, but also bestow on him all kinds of riches and honors.

Pak Chesang looked straight into the eyes of the Japanese King, and said,

"I would rather be a dog or a pig in the land of Silla than the subject of an enemy country, and I would rather endure violence at the hands of my countrymen than enjoy honors and wealth from the hand of their foe."

Furious, the Japanese King ordered a torturer to remove the skin from the soles of Pak's feet, and having cut fresh reeds, made Pak walk upon the sharp edges. He then asked him again.

"Whom do you serve?"

"I serve Silla."

The Japanese King then had an iron plate heated, and having made Pak stand on it, asked again.

"Whom do you serve?"

"I serve Silla."

Pak Chesang never gave in to the wishes of the Japanese King, and was in the end burned alive and beheaded.

Meanwhile, Misahun had landed safely on the shores of Silla, and sent his escort Kang Kuryo to inform the Royal Court of his arrival. King Nulji was amazed and delighted, and went to the southern outskirts of the Palace to meet him, together with all the officials of the Royal Court. When the two brothers met, they took each other's hands and wept. Then the King learned what had happened to Pak. In deep mourning, King Nulji bestowed upon Pak the posthumous honor of *Tae-achan*, "the Great Mountain," and conferred upon his wife the title and rank of the First Lady. To repay his friend's grace, Misahun took the hand of Pak's daughter in marriage.

Pak's wife, meanwhile, was unable to suppress her longing for her husband. Even after his death, she would climb the hill at the *chisul* pass every day to look towards Japan and lament, until one day, her body hardened and became stone – later called the *Mangbuseok*, which means "the stone watching out for her husband."

Her two daughters died together, out of grief for their parents, and it is said that their departed spirits became birds. The place where their spirits ascended has been given the name *Pijo*, or "the bird that flew away." Later, to commemorate the loyalty and devotion of Pak Chesang, the Chisul Memorial Hall was built, and also the Chisul Shrine, in honor of his wife's constancy.

Hwarang Kwisan and Chuhang

During the reign of King Chinpyong (r.579~632) of Silla, there lived a young man named Kwisan.

One day, Kwisan said to his friend Chuhang, "In order for us to live as men of virtue, we must cultivate our minds and bodies. Otherwise, we will not be able to avoid dishonor. Therefore, let us go and seek a wise and enlightened person, and learn the ways of virtue."

At the time, the Buddhist Master Wongwang was staying at a nearby temple, teaching the Dharma of Buddha. Many people, including the King, revered him as a great sage.

Kwisan and Chuhang immediately went to Dharma Master Wongwang and reverently asked him, "We are not monks, but secular students of virtue, very ignorant and without knowledge. Please give us a teaching whereby we may live the rest of our lives."

Dharma Master Wongwang responded to them by saying, "In Buddhism, there are ten precepts for the Bodhisattvas, but if you are to serve as King's vassals, you will probably not be able to abide by them all. There are, however, five precepts that you should live by as laymen. First, serve your King with faithfulness. Second, attend to your parents with utmost piety. Third, let your friendships be based on trust and loyalty. Fourth, never retreat in battle. Fifth, be selective in the taking of life.

Dharma Master Wongwang asked them to practice these five precepts with diligence. By the last precept he meant to teach them that, while killing is inevitable in battle, one should try to practice compassion and avoid killing wherever possible. Kwisan and Chuhang carefully treasured these teachings in their hearts and lived by the five precepts that they received from the Dharma Master.

In the August of the 19th year of King Chinpyong's reign (598), the army of Paekje invaded Silla and laid siege to Fort Amak. King Chinpyong ordered his generals to repel the Paekje forces, and Kwisan and Chuhang took part in the ensuing battle.

The Silla army was successful in defeating Paekje, and they pursued the retreating forces of the enemy. The Paekje forces, however, as they retreated, waited for an opportunity to ambush their pursuers. Some of the Paekje soldiers concealed themselves near a small lake by Mount Chon.

After pursuing the Paekje forces for a while, when the enemy soldiers were no longer in sight, the tired army of Silla was ready to return home. At that moment, the Paekje soldiers who were hiding near Mount Chon suddenly attacked the rear of Silla army, where Kwisan's father Muon had been assigned. Learning of the ambush, Kwisan reflected, "Since I have learned from Dharma Master Wongwang that a warrior must never retreat in battle, how can I run away?" He then threw himself into the middle of the Paekje forces and cut down several tens of the enemy soldiers. He allowed his father to escape by giving him his own horse, and fought with all his might beside his friend Chuhang.

Having witnessed Kwisan's valor, the Silla soldiers regained their morale and began to fight back against Paekje. It is said that the Paekje forces who had launched the ambush were completely defeated in the battle that followed. The battlefield was covered with the bodies of Paekje troops, and not a single one of their soldiers or horses returned home. Kwisan and Chuhang were heavily wounded in the battle and died on the return journey. The King and his officials went all the way to the battlefield at Ana to mourn the fate of the two young warriors and to pay their respects.

Through the honorable deaths of Kwisan and Chuhang, the Five Secular Precepts by which they had lived became widely known, and from then on served as the guiding ethos of the *Hwarang-do*. The *Hwarang-do* was a company of youths in the Silla kingdom who devoted themselves to cultivation of the mind and body. Each separate *Hwarang-do* was placed under the leadership of one *Hwarang* and many *Nangdos*. *Hwarangs* were generally the sons of aristocratic families, who were trustworthy, sociable and of good appearance. They were selected on the recommendation of the *Nangdos*. Each *Hwarang* had around 300 to 1000 *Nangdos* under his command. Throughout the Silla period, there were about 200 *Hwarangs* in total.

Hwarangs and *Nangdos* sought out famous mountains and rivers where they could train in martial arts and cultivate their minds together. Their friendship and loyalty to one another created a spirit of self-sacrifice for a greater cause, which in turn became the spirit of the age in which they lived. According to the biographies of different *Hwarangs* in the *History of Three Kingdoms* (1281), *Hwarangs*, *Nangdos*, and even ordinary soldiers were unafraid to sacrifice their lives in order to defend the country, since they firmly believed that it was an honor to die in battle.

The spirit of *Hwarang* shone most brilliantly at the time when the conflict between the three ancient kingdoms, Koguryo, Paekje, and Silla, was at its worst, during the 6th and 7th centuries AD. The contribution of this group of young patriots to the defense of Silla was indispensable, as their nation was in a state of perpetual crisis, being at war with both Koguryo and Paekje for over 100 years. In any emergency, they were immediately assigned to the army and sent to war. After an initial training period, they served as officials in the government or in the army. *Hwarang-do* was a very chivalrous organization, and its members did not hesitate to help the weak. At times, in order to look after the security of their society, they took on the duty of patrolling the towns at night. According to the *Chronicles of Hwarang* written by Kim Daemun, all the brave warriors and worthy officials of Silla were once *Hwarangs*.

The spirit of *Hwarang* was a foundation which enabled the small nation of Silla to defeat the stronger countries of Paekje and Koguryo and achieve the unification of Korea, which was the ultimate goal of the period.

The *Hwarangs* were armed with the Five Secular Precepts: faithfulness to the king, utmost piety to parents, trust and loyalty to friends, unflinching bravery in battle, and prudence in the taking of life. They possessed a genuine love for their country and the people who lived in it. For their country and people, they were willing to sacrifice their lives without hesitation, true patriots indeed. Their pure and sincere loyalty to their country both moved and molded the spirit of the Silla people whom they defended. And so, through the combined power of their loyal spirits, the people of Silla were able to make Korea into one nation.

The Pure Heart of Sadaham

During the reign of King Chinhung (r.534~576), the kingdom of Silla was constantly at war with the neighboring kingdom of Kaya. Kaya was like a thorn in its side, for whenever Silla tried to advance to the north, Kaya would always oppose it. In order to unify Korea, Silla would first have to subjugate Kaya.

King Chinhung ordered General Yi Sabu to lead this campaign. Kaya was a powerful ancient kingdom which had conquered the smaller kingdoms around it, and its influence reached all the way to Paekje and Japan. At one point, it had possessed the most advanced technology in iron manufacture in East Asia. Its military power was therefore not to be taken lightly.

In those days, there lived in Silla a young man named Sadaham, who lived to be of great benefit to the kingdom. He was a descendent of King Namil, and his father was a high-ranking official. He was praised by many people for his noble ideals and appearance, and his integrity. Many recommended that he be made a *Hwarang*, a role which he modestly declined for a long time. When he finally became a *Hwarang*, close to one thousand *Nangdos* were under his leadership, and all had great respect for him.

When General Yi Sabu was about to go to war with Kaya, young Sadaham, who was at the time only 15 or 16 years old, also volunteered for the war. He begged the General to let him fight and sacrifice his life for his country. Even battle-hardened veterans had anxieties about war with Kaya, and many felt that it was too soon for Sadaham to fight in the war, even though he was a *Hwarang* whose code was to never retreat in battle.

In response, Sadaham expressed his earnest wish to participate, saying,

"Why should my youth be a hindrance to my defending the country?"

Even King Chinhung was surprised by Sadaham's wish. However, Sadaham's patriotism was so admirable that the King permitted him to fight in the war. Sadaham began to make preparations, and eventually took up his position as an aide to the Commander-in-Chief. When it was announced that Sadaham was going to war, many *Hwarangs* and *Nangdos* volunteered to serve under his command. This influx of new recruits greatly boosted the morale of the Silla army.

When they finally reached Kaya's border, the confronting enemy forces retreated into a fortified position and would not come out. As General Yi Sabu was discussing with his officers how to proceed, Sadaham came before him and announced his plan.

"Sir, I volunteer to lead the vanguard in a direct assault."

"Your request is admirable, but you may be too …"

Before General Yi Sabu could refuse Sadaham because of his inexperience, Sadaham began to plead with the General.

"General, I implore you to grant this request. Since sacrificing one's life for the country is an honorable deed, what is there for me to fear? Although I lack experience, if I fight with all my strength, I am sure to prevail."

General Yi Sabu was moved by Sadaham's indomitable spirit, and so Sadaham led the vanguard in an attack on the enemy's position. While the Kaya soldiers were panicking from this unexpected action, Sadaham established control of the fort. It was a great victory for Silla.

When Sadaham returned in triumph, the King commended his victory and rewarded him with 300 Kayan prisoners to be his slaves. Sadaham, however, freed them all. The King then tried to show his gratitude to Sadaham by offering him land. But Sadaham even tried to decline this as well.

When the King strongly urged Sadaham to accept the land, he was no longer able to refuse and finally asked the King, "If your highness wishes to reward me with some land, please give me the most barren land in the region of Ilchon." Realizing that Sadaham really had no desire to enrich himself, the King could only follow his wish.

Sadaham had a very close friend named Mukwanrang. In their youth, they had sworn to die in battle together. However, Mugwanrang, who was not in good health, fell ill and died soon afterwards.

Sadaham was stricken with grief. He stopped eating and lamented day and night. Eventually, within seven days of his friend's passing, he also died. At the time, he was only 17 years old.

Even by the standards of the day, and even for a *Hwarang* who had sworn loyalty to his friend, Sadaham's decision to die was probably not an easy one. However, he gave his life in order to honor the promise he had made to his friend.

Sadaham's heart was as pure as the untouched snow. It may have been due to such pure-hearted loyalty and friendship that Silla was able to unify the ancient kingdoms of Korea, and continued to rule Korea for a thousand years, an unprecedented length of time for any Eastern dynasty.

Let No Grass Grow Where I Am Buried

General Choi Yong (1316~1388), who served as a military commander during the Koryo Dynasty, was a man of great loyalty and strength of will. When facing an enemy in battle, he remained calm, showing no sign of fear even beneath a hail of arrows. Consequently, he won many victories and never suffered a defeat.

When he was sixteen, his father Choi Wonjik passed away. Before he died, he instructed his son to treat gold as if it were stone.

Choi Yong always cherished his father's dying words deep in his heart, and never concerned himself with material wealth. His house was shabby and in poor repair, but he was content with it. He was so thrifty with food and clothes that sometimes he ran out of it altogether. Even though he held the position of Prime Minister and Supreme General, and was for a long time in command of the entire military, he never accepted a bribe. Although he remained in control of the armed forces until his death, only a few people from his army knew his appearance. This was because he did not give preference or promotions to people who were connected to him on the basis of their personal relationship.

At the time, Yi In-im and Yim Kyon-mi were in charge of government appointments, and used their positions for personal gain. They accepted bribes from many people and recommended them for preferment in return. As a result, anyone with money could find employment as a government official.

One day, a young scholar came to Choi Yong seeking government office. Choi Yong said to him, "If you were a merchant or maker of mattocks or shoes, you could easily get a position." The young man was confused and asked, "What do you mean?" Choi Yong replied, "These days, I hear that official positions are bartered in exchange for money. As scholars such as yourself do not have much money, it would surely be easier for a craftsman or a merchant to obtain a government post."

When Choi Yong began to oversee the appointment of government personnel, he employed only those people with talent or merit enough for the positions, and had no hesitation in passing over those who lacked the necessary qualifications.

One day, when Yi In-im was Prime Minister, Choi Yong asked him, "When our nation is in such great difficulty, how can you, the Prime Minister of the country, care only for increasing your personal fortune?" Yi could say nothing to Choi Yong in reply.

In 1388, King Wu ordered General Yi Songgye to take the army and recover the Liaodong area from China, who had captured it from Koguryo many centuries before. General Yi Songgye went out with 50,000 men to undertake the mission, but turned back at Wihwa Island, and having dethroned the King, set himself up as ruler. He then had King Wu sent into exile.

In order to remove Choi Yong, who was greatly respected by the people, Yi Songgye's supporters laid false charges against him, claiming that he had secretly accumulated vast wealth by dishonest means.

At his execution, he left behind these words, "If I was ever greedy in my life, let grass grow over where I am buried. But if I never acted out of greed, may the grass never grow there."

According to his words, his grave still remains barren after more than 500 years.

Chong Mongju and
the 72 Wise Men of Tumundong

Chong Mongju (1337~1392) was a government minister and scholar during the Koryo dynasty (918~1392). In 1357, at the age of 21, he passed the state examination, and three years later achieved first place in the literary examinations. In the year 1367, as an official in the Ministry of Culture and Education, he was appointed to the co-professorship at Songkyunkwan National University, and later went on to attain the highest post in the Ministry.

The closing years of the Koryo dynasty had been a turbulent period, with endless harassments by Japanese pirates, and revolts in the military. At this point, a new party called the *Sinjin Sadaebu* entered the political arena. Comprising the best educated of the government's officials, they originally emerged under King Kong-min (r. 1351~1374) with the revival of the State Examination and the founding of Songkyunkwan National University. The *Sinjin Sadaebu* steadily grew in influence against the rival Pro-*Yuan* and aristocratic *Kwonmun* parties, and eventually came to dominate the political landscape of late Koryo. As the power of government weakened and the ideological tide began to turn, the *Sinjin Sadaebu* split into two factions – one dedicated to the preservation of the old order, the other seeking to replace it. The former faction was led by Chong Mongju, and aimed at reviving the failing Koryo dynasty. General Yi Songgye, whose power and fame were increasing day by day, was the central figure of the opposing faction, which planned to establish the new dynasty of Choson.

Chong Mongju was the teacher and chief counselor to King Kong-yang, and was assisting in the administration of the state, while Yi Songgye marched across the country from battlefield to battlefield, leaving brilliant victories behind him. As far as the people were concerned, the real authority lay in the hands of Yi and his followers, since they controlled the army. Chong Mongju and Yi Songgye were old acquaintances, having studied under the same master, and had pledged their lives for each other as comrades-in-arms. When Yi was waging his campaign against the Japanese pirates, he owed a number of his victories to the advice and assistance of Chong.

General Yi came from a family of warriors, but also possessed a yearning for literature and academic study. Therefore, he had a special admiration for Chong Mongju, who excelled in both war and literary pursuits. Moreover, as companions in battle, who had vowed to share the same fate on many occasions, they had developed a strong bond of mutual trust and friendship.

In their opinions on social reform, however, Yi Songgye and Chong Mongju could not have been further apart. The society Chong hoped to re-create was conceived firmly within the framework of old Koryo, while Yi wished to abolish Koryo's very name. Consequently, their friendship was put under considerable strain as the conflict between the supporters of these separate views intensified. Yi Songgye tried to persuade Chong Mongju to join him, even though it would cause delay to his plans. Since Chong Mongju was generally regarded as the nation's foremost scholar, and commanded the absolute trust of the people, it would have been difficult to give the revolution an appearance of legitimacy without his support.

Yi Pang-won, the fifth son of Yi Songgye, invited Chong Mongju to his house when he saw that the scholar was proving an obstacle to the founding of the new Choson dynasty. He served him wine, and recited the following *sijo*, or three-verse ode, in order to probe his true intentions.

To go this way or that way, what is the difference?

It is wrong for the arrowroots on the ancient mountain to twist and twine?

We too may change our course, and live on in happiness, even for a hundred years.

Replying with another *sijo*, Chong expressed his loyalty to Koryo:

Even though I die and die again, a hundred, or a thousand times,

Though my bones become dust and clay, whether I have a soul or not,

My single, unwavering devotion to the *nim*[6], will never change, nor be turned aside.

Through this *sijo*, later entitled *Singleness of Heart*, Chong revealed that even if he were to die a hundred times, his loyalty and devotion as a subject of Koryo would never falter. After listening to his *sijo*, Pang-won realized that Chong would never change his mind. Although he greatly regretted it, he felt that Chong would have to be removed. Although Yi Songgye had warned his son never to take any extreme action against Chong, as he was his close friend, Pang-won sent for his colleague Yi Jiran and told him of his plan to get rid of Chong. Yi Jiran was greatly distressed, and said, "The mandate of Heaven is already with you, general. Our plan of action will not go astray because of a single person; why then do you wish to slay this great sage of our nation? Even though I am an ignorant fellow, sorely lacking in wisdom, I could never bring myself to do such a thing."

Pang-won knew Jiran spoke the truth, but he felt the revolt would not be swiftly accomplished unless Chong were removed, and that the present

---

[6] The word *nim* literally means one's beloved, cherished one, and it here symbolizes the King and the Koryo dynasty which Chong Mongju revered.

opportunity to do so could not be missed. He therefore summoned his private confidant, Cho Yonggyu, and ordered, "Go to the armory with all speed, and proceed to the Seonji Bridge with an iron mace. Conceal yourself there, and when Chong Mongju passes by, beat him to death there and then, neither speaking to him nor listening to his words. Then, return to me and confirm that it is done."

Without hesitating, Cho Yonggyu hurried to the Seonji Bridge as Pang-won had ordered. As he was leaving Yi Songgye's house, Chong sensed that his life was drawing to an end. The recent words and actions of Yi Songgye and Pang-won clearly indicated that he would soon be silenced. Chong was greatly saddened, grieving not so much for the loss of his life as for the future of his country. Nevertheless, he knew that there was little he could do. Tears flowed in silence along the furrows of the timeworn face of Koryo's loyal subject.

As he was immersed in these sorrowful thoughts, his horse drew near the Seonji Bridge. Suddenly, a large figure with an iron mace entered his vision, and an understanding of what was to come flashed through his mind. Chong calmly ordered his horse to stop, and turning to his personal attendant following behind, he quietly told him, "There is danger in the air today. Although my course has already been decided, there is no need for you to suffer too. Leave this place, quickly."

Chong's attendant, Kim Kyongjo, was the son of Kim Kuju, who had served as Prime Minister under King Kong-min. Kim Kyongjo was an upright man, and had long possessed a deep respect for Chong. Upon hearing his resolve and concern for his safety, his tears began to pour like rain.

"How could I wish to live on in peace when you will suffer? No matter what befalls, I will serve you until the very end."

With these words Kim followed him, even though Chong strongly urged against it. Having no choice, Chong sent away the other servants and permitted Kim to follow. He urged on his horse, and as he arrived at the bridge, the figure he had previously seen ran towards him and tried to hit him on the back of the head. As this happened, Kim quickly embraced Chong as the metal mace ruthlessly struck him down. Kim fell, coughing up blood, and died there and then. Not long afterwards Chong also fell from his horse and gave up his life.

Soon afterwards, a bamboo tree began to grow on the bridge where Chong had fallen. From this, the bridge was given a new name of *Seonjuk* (Bamboo of Virtue)[7] to replace its original name, *Seonji* (Land of Virtue).

To this day, traces of the blood shed by Chong still remain, reminding all who pass of the loyal and patriotic spirit that once dwelt in this heroic man.

Upon hearing the news of his friend's death, Yi Songgye reproved Pang-won bitterly. "You fool! Now that you have killed the father of the nation, what will the people say to me?"

The new dynasty of Choson was eventually founded, and Yi Pang-won became its third king (Taejong). Since he had great reverence for the devotion of Chong Mongju, he conferred upon him the title of Prime Minister, the highest of posthumous titles, Minister of Knowledge, and Minister of Loyalty.

One hundred and twenty-five years later, at the petition of the National University of Choson, the Royal Court enshrined Chong Mongju in the Hall of Confucius, a building dedicated to the wise men of successive ages, and raised a monument where he was buried. Respecting his will not to serve two sovereigns, the inscription mentions only the offices he held under Koryo, omitting the posthumous titles given to him by Choson. Yi Pang-won, who had Chong Mongju removed, and the new government of the Choson dynasty, which Chong had opposed at the cost of his life, both accepted him as a loyal subject and revered him as a model of faithfulness for future generations of every persuasion and belief.

As Koryo fell and the new Choson dynasty rose to take its place, the

---

[7] Bamboo, with its straight stem and evergreen leaves, symbolized immovable loyalty.

scholars of *Sinjin Sadaebu* who had striven for the revival of Koryo by the side of Chong Mongju, all resigned their positions and took sanctuary in the valley of Tumundong, stating that it was against their duty as scholars to serve two sovereigns. From then on, in the minds of the people, Tumundong became a symbol for the denial of the new Choson government's legitimacy.

"Every true patriot is in Tumundong," men would say, "And those who are responsible for the present disturbances are all the traitors of Koryo." With the people opposed to them in their hearts, it was proving increasingly difficult for Yi Songgye and his party to justify the founding of Choson. Ministers of the Choson Court visited Tumundong and employed all manner of threats to bring about some kind of agreement between them, but the scholars were unmoved.

The Royal Court of Choson eventually came to the conclusion that they would never be persuaded, and issued an ultimatum: "If you continue to resist, this whole village will be burnt down. Elect to remain here and die, or become a subject of Choson. You have only one day."

The last 72 loyal members of the five-hundred-year-long Koryo dynasty resisted to the end, and either died at Tumundong or were scattered to the rest of the country. For their decision to die as the subjects of Koryo rather than share in the honor of founding Choson, these members of the *Sinjin Sadaebu* were later known as the 72 Wise Men of Tumundong.

They differed strikingly from the *Kwonmun* aristocracy, which also fell with the Koryo dynasty. As membership of the *Kwonmun* was determined by blood ties and family lineage, when the basis of their power fell, the *Kwonmuns* could do nothing to help themselves, as their talent was extremely feeble. The merit and virtues of the 72 Wise Men of Tumundong, however, had been forged on the anvil of the state examinations. With their firm grasp of Confucian ethics and wisdom, they were the intellectual elite of their day, and the Royal Court of Choson was in great need of them. Faced with the enticements of wealth and fame, they made the ultimate sacrifice out of loyalty to Koryo. Hence they could be called true patriots, each of whom chose their own fate. Since they were the followers of a ruined dynasty, proper records of their actions have all disappeared, and only the briefest accounts of their lives remain, in chance tales and anecdotes. Their spirit, however, founded upon respect for the traditional Confucian order and the importance of duty and principle, faithfulness and righteousness, has been passed down throughout the generations, and became a spiritual foundation and source of wonder even to the scholars of Choson.

Kyonghoe Pavilion of Kyongbok Palace

Prime Minister Hwang Hee

Hwang Hee (1363~1452), who served as Prime Minister during the reign of King Sejong the Great, is thought to have been the greatest and most accomplished government minister of the Choson period. He devoted sixty-one years of his life to serving the state, of which twenty-four were spent as Prime Minister.

As a man he was kind and generous, and also thoughtful and self-controlled. He was known for his honesty and fair-dealing, and for his devotion to his country and parents. As he grew older and rose to higher positions, his way of life became even more humble. Even when he turned 90, he still devoted himself to study. When his vision began to fail in his old age, he continued to read books, using each of his eyes in turn.

When he was a young man, he once occupied the lowest government post in the Choksong area. One day, as he was resting briefly on the road on his way to Seoul, he saw a farmer with two cows plowing the land.

He approached the farmer and asked him, "Which of the cows is better?" The farmer, however, did not respond to Hwang Hee, but simply stared at him for a while. He then continued to plow the land.

Having been ignored by the farmer, Hwang Hee felt embarrassed and went back to rest under a tree. When he was about to leave, the farmer came up to him, and whispered in his ear, "The cow on the left hand side is better."

Curious, Hwang Hee asked him, "Why are you telling me as if it is a secret?" The farmer replied apologetically, "Even though they are animals, they are the same way as humans. If one cow is better, the other cow is worse. If I were to let the other cow hear this, it would hurt its feelings."

Hearing the farmer's words, Hwang Hee had a great awakening. From that day on, he never talked about the good or bad qualities of other people without careful consideration.

When he held the second highest position in the civil service, he brought a young servant from Hwanghae Province to perform errands for his children while they were studying.

This servant was eventually able to recite by heart the Confucian classics that he overheard as he worked outside the room where Hwang's children were reading them aloud. Hwang Hee was so impressed by the servant's talents that he wanted to make him a free man.

In order to free him – which was against both law and custom at the time – he had to send him far away. When he left, he said to him, "Do not speak of this to anyone else. Move far away, and find a great scholar to study under. With persistent effort, you will be able to succeed." He bade him farewell, telling him never to return.

Ten years later, when Hwang Hee was Prime Minister, five or six people who passed the civil service examination that year all requested to visit him. One of the young men dismounted his horse outside the house, and as soon as he entered the gate, he kneeled down on the ground before Hwang Hee.

Hwang Hee was surprised, and asked him, "Why do you show me such respect?" The young official spoke the name he had used when he had served him as a child, and Hwang Hee recognized him as the servant he had sent away ten years before.

Hwang Hee did not let him speak any more, but entertained him well. Later he called for the young scholar and quietly told him, "I am afraid that if others find out about your background, your career may suffer. So please take care." The young man was deeply moved by Hwang Hee's kindness. He later rose to a high position in the government and earned much honor and respect.

Even when Hwang Hee became Prime Minister, he lived in an old thatched hut without proper fences. When King Sejong heard about this, he sent a message to the Minister of Industry, ordering him to build fences around Hwang Hee's house in secret. The minister called together several skilled builders and went to Hwang Hee's house late at night. They made haste to finish their task before daybreak.

While they were in the middle of their work, a section of the fence fell down, and Hwang Hee woke up because of the noise. He came out of his hut and asked, "What are you doing at my house at this late hour?" Being confronted by Hwang Hee, the Minister of Industry was forced to tell him about the King's command.

The next day, Hwang Hee went before the King and said,

"Although your servant is the Prime Minister, there are nonetheless many poor people who live without fences. Please withdraw your royal command to build fences around my house."

King Sejong and his officials were all moved by Hwang Hee's integrity, and some even shed tears upon hearing his request.

One day, as King Sejong was paying visits outside the palace, it occurred to him to stop by Hwang Hee's house, as he heard that he lived in the area. So, he altered his plans and visited Hwang Hee's house unexpectedly.

When the King was led through the other houses in the neighborhood to an unusually small and rundown dwelling, he was surprised. He thought to himself, "How could the house of the Prime Minister, who holds the highest position after the king himself, be in such condition?"

When he entered the house, he was even more surprised, as the room contained only a threadbare mat and a patched blanket resting on top of an old chest. Sejong, worried that Hwang Hee might be embarrassed, quickly hid his expression of surprise and joked, "I suppose, when you are lying down on it, this mat must be convenient for scratching your back."

As soon as he returned to the palace, King Sejong called for Hwang Hee, and asked him, "How can a country maintain its dignity when the Prime Minister's house is in such a sorry state?" he asked him. "Is it because your salary is insufficient?"

Hwang Hee replied, "No, Your Majesty, it is quite sufficient. But how can a civil servant live a life of extravagance? As for my clothing, it is enough for it to be within the bounds of etiquette. And a house is good enough if it can keep out the wind and the rain."

Sejong said, "Even so, your situation seems extreme. Obtain all things of which you may be in need, and I will pay for them."

Hwang Hee persisted in refusing to accept the King's gifts and said, "Your majesty, forgive me if I dare to decline your generosity. But there are many things in this country that require your attention. So, please do not turn your mind to such a small matter."

On another occasion, during the winter, Hwang Hee said his wife, "Dear wife, please pull apart these clothes and wash them for me. If we dry them over night and sew them back together, I shall be able to wear them tomorrow morning when I go back to the palace." In the old days, traditional Korean winter clothes had stretches of cotton sewn inside them. When they were washed, the pieces were separated and the cotton wadding was removed.

Prime Minister Hwang Hee had only one set of winter clothes. As he was reading that evening in his underwear, a messenger came and announced, "Your Excellency, the King has ordered you to return to the palace as quickly as possible."

His wife panicked and said, "My husband, we are in trouble! The King has ordered you to return to the palace, but you have nothing to wear."

Hwang Hee thought briefly, then said, "Well, there is nothing we can do. Why don't you give me the cotton instead?" She replied, "What cotton?"

Hwang said, "Well, you must still have the cotton lining that you took from the clothes before you washed them." His wife said, "You are mad. How can you wear plain cotton before the King?" He replied, "Well, what am I supposed to do then? I cannot refuse to go to the palace since it is the King's order, and I cannot wear my official clothes on top of my underwear. So, bring me the cotton."

Hwang Hee wrapped himself in the cotton lining, and asked his wife for some thick thread. When his wife finished stitching together all the cotton from his shirt and britches, Hwang Hee put on his official clothes and hastily made his way to the palace.

King Sejong had gathered together all his ministers in order to discuss how to repel the Japanese pirates who had invaded the Southern Coast. During their discussion, King Sejong noticed something white sticking out of Hwang Hee's official clothes. The King assumed it was wool, and thought it odd that Prime Minister Hwang, a man known for his frugality, possessed such expensive clothes.

After the meeting, the King ordered Hwang Hee to approach him and said, "I know your integrity and simple way of life are exemplary, and your reputation reaches the Heavens themselves, but how is it that you have come today wearing woolen clothes?"

Hwang Hee was embarrassed and struggled to reply. "Your majesty, this is not wool but cotton."

"Cotton?" the King replied, "Why are you wearing cotton?"

"I have one pair of winter clothes, your Majesty. And today, as I went home early, I had my wife pull them apart to wash them, and…"

"How can this be?" Sejong exclaimed, "Prime Minister, come a little closer." And the King felt the cotton sticking out from beneath Hwang Hee's official clothes. Sejong then declared, "Prime minister, your frugality is excessive. How can you pass the winter with only one set of clothes?"

He then ordered his attendant to provide Hwang Hee with ten rolls of silk. With a look of surprise on his face, Hwang Hee then said,

"Your Majesty, please withdraw your command. Many people in this country are suffering from malnutrition and poverty as a result of the continuing famine. In times like this, how could a prime minister wear silk around his body? Since cotton clothes are more than sufficient, please accept my way of dressing."

King Sejong said, "You speak like the Hwang Hee I know. I am embarrassed to be wearing these royal clothes." He then withdrew his order to provide Hwang Hee with silk.

Nongae, the "Righteous Rock"

Nongae's family name was Chu, and her father's name was Talmun. Her father was an impoverished nobleman who, as his ancestors had done, made a living by teaching the Confucian classics to local children.

He married a lady from the Pak family in Pongjol village. They lived happily together and had a son named Taeryong, whom they raised with much love and care. However, at the age of 15, he suddenly fell ill and died. Since they had no other offspring, the couple went to a temple on the famous Changan Mountain to pray for another child. As a result of their devoted prayers, Nongae was born.

Even when she was little, Nongae was well known for her beauty and great filial piety. She was also highly intelligent and accomplished in scholarly pursuits, and often taught her father's students when he was away.

Since in her youth she was very beautiful and had an air of nobility, her father's students often made improper advances to her. She maintained an attitude of dignity and did not say anything to them, but one day gave them a piece of paper with the following poem, written in Chinese characters:

A flower blossoms high upon a branch, and men cannot reach it.
The tall grass grows thick on the ground, and dogs cannot pass through it.

In this poem, Nongae was comparing herself to a flower that blossomed in a high and serene place, and the students to dogs tumbling in the thick foliage beneath. When the meaning of the poem dawned on them, the students were very embarrassed. It is said that those who read the poem never troubled her again.

Even when she was young, her devotion to her parents was exemplary. From dawn till dusk, she never rested from her duties, and would not even eat until her mother and father had finished their meal. To the young Nongae, happiness meant making her parents happy, even if it was by doing something as simple as bringing them wild berries or herbs she had gathered.

In 1587, her father fell ill. After being bedridden for the entire winter, his health was in a critical condition. Nongae did everything she could to help, and even bit her finger and held it above her father's mouth[8], but her efforts were of no use and her father passed away.

All of Nongae's misfortunes began with the death of her father. Once he was gone, she passed into the care of her uncle, a man notorious for his disorderly conduct and riotous living. Upon becoming her guardian, her uncle made a journey to visit a wealthy proprietor called Kim Punghon, pretending that he was concerned for the welfare of his brother's family, when in fact he was hoping to obtain money from Kim to support his debauchery. Kim, for his part, wanted to buy Nongae as a wife for his backward son. Their intentions were well suited to one another, and it did not take them long to settle the terms of the deal. In exchange for a Four Pillars Box[9] from Kim Punghon, Nongae's uncle received 300 *nyang* of brass coins, 3 rolls of cotton cloth, and the deed to 3 *majigi* (about half an acre) of land. He then proceeded to spend it all immediately before returning to his hometown.

---

[8] In old Korea, it was believed that blood from one's finger could heal those who were near death.

[9] The "Four Pillars" or *saju* box was a traditional wedding item sent from the groom's family to the bride's family. It contained the year, month, day and hour of the groom's birth, which was used to calculate the most auspicious day for the wedding. It was thus a symbol of the acceptance of marriage.

Later, however, under growing pressure from Kim Punghon to fulfill his part of the deal, Nongae's uncle placed the Four Pillars Box in the hands Nongae's mother, and disappeared. Kim, meanwhile, had determined an auspicious day for the wedding, and accordingly sent word to Nongae's family. To Nongae and her mother, who were completely unaware of what had been agreed between the two men, this came like a bolt of lightning from a clear summer sky, and they fled to the house of her mother's parents.

When Kim sent his servants with a carriage to the hometown of Nongae on the day of the wedding, she was nowhere to be found. Having wasted his time and money, Kim filed a complaint with the local magistrate, Choi Kyonghoe, against Nongae and her mother. The magistrate had them arrested and brought in for questioning.

When he spoke to Nongae and her mother, however, he realized that they were innocent and that the uncle had sold Nongae to Kim without her knowledge, before disappearing himself. But even though she was unaware of what Nongae's uncle had done, the mother had nevertheless received the Four Pillars Box, and was thus technically in breach of the agreement. She was therefore sentenced to serve as a government slave for five years. Nongae thought that she herself deserved to endure this sentence in her mother's place, and requested the magistrate to allow this, pleading to him, "My mother is old and weak. Since it is impossible for her to serve the government for five years as a slave, please permit me to serve in her place."

The magistrate was moved by Nongae's tearful pleas and devotion, and cancelled the sentence altogether, judging the two women innocent. Now that her uncle had fled, however, Nongae and her mother had no means of surviving. Aware of their wretched situation, the magistrate Choi Kyong-hoe allowed them to stay at his own house. His wife was gravely ill at the time, and Nongae and her mother nursed and cared for her. Nongae tended to the magistrate and his wife with great thoughtfulness. Knowing that her own death was near, the magistrate's wife recommended to Choi that he marry the wise and virtuous Nongae.

After several years had passed since the death of the magistrate's wife, Nongae became his new wife, and their affection for each other grew deeper by the day.

A little later, Choi was appointed as the magistrate of Mujang village, and Choi and Nongae went to live there. However, after only six months had passed, the Imjin War (1592-1598) broke out. At this time, the villagers and townspeople throughout the country were rallying around local leaders to form volunteer guerilla forces. Having realized the peril of their situation, they were determined to defend their country. The magistrate Choi gathered together the young men of his town, and joined the volunteer defense forces as commander of the Kyongsang Army.

In October 1592, 30,000 of Japan's best-trained soldiers, led by the Commander Simazu Yoshihiro, surrounded the city of Chinju and laid siege to it. The resistance of the 3,800 Korean troops defending it, however, was staunch and fierce. In the end, after a week of desperate assault and resolute defense, the Japanese commanders called off the attack, and the decision was taken to raise the siege and withdraw.

However, the Japanese returned in the following summer to avenge their defeat before the city. Kato Kiyomasa, Konish Ukinaga, and Ukita Hideie, the very best of their commanders, invaded Chinju once again with a force of 80,000 men.

On the 20th June, the vanguard divisions arrived, and when the main division was in place on the next day, the Japanese completed their preparations for attack, beginning their renewed offensive on the 22nd of June. Black clouds moving in from the south cast darkness everywhere, and rain began to fall, signaling the onset of the monsoon season.

The Japanese sent their regiments into battle by turns, never slackening in their aggression by day or night. The soldiers and the people of Chinju, however, held on with almost superhuman strength. Nongae had formed an army composed of women, called the Nangja Army, who carried stones to the defenders on the walls, and boiled water in cauldrons to pour over the enemy as they climbed up.

Amid torrential rain and unending assaults by the enemy, the south-eastern wall was breached on 28th June. By the heroic efforts of General Hwang, the waves of enemy soldiers were pushed back momentarily and the walls were repaired, but unfortunately the General was hit in the forehead by a musket ball, and so died in this last desperate attempt to save the city. On the night of 29th June, the southern-western walls were breached again, and collapsed before the Japanese army, which entered like a swarm of bees. The city had fallen.

As the Japanese army poured in, Nongae's husband, Magistrate Choi Kyonghoe and the other commanders retreated to the Choksok pavilion at the southern wall of the city, which overlooked the Nam River. After bowing towards the north, the capital and their king, with the tears streaming down their faces, they recited a poem that they had prepared for this final moment.

> At the Choksok Pavilion, the three of us stand drinking wine,
> And point to the flowing river with smiles.
> To this side and that, the waters of the Nam River surge onwards,
> As long as the river does not run dry, our souls will not fade away.

With this, they threw themselves into the water below, offering their lives in a final act of devotion to the country they had sought to defend.

The Japanese had no mercy, and left not so much as a cow, dog or chicken alive in the city. Of at least sixty thousand Koreans who lost their lives in the Second Battle of Chinju, most were killed in the massacre that followed the city's capture. Having heard of the atrocities carried out by the victors, Nongae, who had escaped with other women before the city fell, was filled with sorrow and indignation.

Intending to celebrate their victory at Choksok Pavilion on the 7th of July, the Japanese army put up notices on every street corner requesting the services of *kisaengs*, or professional female entertainers. Having seen these, Nongae felt it was a heaven-sent opportunity for her to avenge her country. She found a *kisaeng* named Suan, told her of her plans, and then had her own name recorded in the register of *kisaengs*. The seventh day of July finally arrived, and all the Japanese commanders who had participated in the battle of Chinju gathered at Choksok Pavilion. Nongae appeared at the party wearing extravagant dress, with a ring on each of her fingers.

With the help of the other *kiseangs* at the party, she was able to approach General Keyamura, who had led the siege of the city. Nongae served cup after cup of wine to the swaggering Keyamura, so that he would become drunk. Smiling and dancing in front of the intoxicated general, she gradually led him away from the party to a rock high above the Nam River. Captivated, he came closer and closer to Nongae, step by step. When they were both standing on the edge of the rock, she embraced the Japanese general with all her strength, locking her hands together with the rings, and then jumped into the river with the Japanese general.

Fifteen days into the monsoon season, the Nam River was flowing with uncontrollable force. Nongae disappeared into the deep and seething waters, dragging down Keyamura in her arms. Thus she ended her young and beautiful life, at the age of 19.

To Koreans, Nongae's spirit of defiance and the story of her noble sacrifice represent the ultimate expression of virtue and loyalty. A monument and shrine have been built to commemorate her patriotism, and the rock from which she threw herself was named the Righteous Rock (Kor. *Uiam*). This also became her posthumous title, awarded by the Yemungwan, or Office of Royal Records, and has been identified with Nongae ever since. Several years later, the magistrate of Chinju left a fitting inscription for Nongae's monument, urging everyone to emulate her virtue.

> Even when one's country is under invasion and in turmoil and distress, it is not easy to sacrifice one's life rather than live on in humiliation. It is not easy even for a true patriot, and yet she saw her death as a means of returning to the origin. How bright and moving it is! When I think of her final act, its dignity and righteousness shine as clearly as the stars and the sun. She was glorious indeed…Since many people have reverently expressed a desire to follow her example, with deference, I hereby leave a record of her righteous name for future generations.

To Nongae, who fully realized the practice of filial devotion, virtue and loyalty, throughout her brief and tumultuous life, Byon Yongro, one of the greatest poets of Korea, dedicated the following poem.

> A noble indignation
> Fiercer than religious fervor;
> A burning passion
> Stronger than love.
>
> A soul redder than the poppies
> Flowed upon waves bluer than the cornflower.
>
> The fair eye-lashes trembled;
> The pomegranate lips kissed Death.

A soul redder than the poppies
Flowed upon waves bluer than the cornflower.

The flowing river will remain forever blue;
The beautiful soul will remain forever red.

A soul redder than the poppies
Flowed upon waves bluer than the cornflower.

The Meaning of Chung

Since the founding of Korea as a nation in 2333 BC[10], *Hyo* (filial devotion) and *Chung* (loyalty) have been the two most important moral values that guided the minds and spirits of the Korean people. *Hyo* and *Chung* could be compared to the two faces of a coin, as they are concepts which cannot be thought of separately. *Chung* is usually understood to mean loyalty to one's country and its ruler. However, the word *Chung* contains the broader meaning of acting with a sincere mind towards oneself and others, as well as one's country.

The virtue of *Hyo* is respect and gratefulness towards our parents, who brought us into the world and raised us. Koreans believe that devotion to one's country is in fact a way of fulfilling one's true filial duty, for *Hyo* is the basis on which people love their family, society, and the nation. In other words, *Hyo* is the inner core of *Chung* and *Chung* is a broader expression of *Hyo*.

During the period of the Three Kingdoms, Buddhist Master Wongwang of Silla gave the *Hwarangs* Five Secular Precepts to live by. The first precept was "to serve the King with faithfulness." Here the word "King" does not refer to a single, isolated individual, but to the one who leads and represents a country's government. The *Hwarangs'* oath to "serve the King with faithfulness" was an expression of their wish to help the King's government rule justly, to the best of their abilities, and for the benefit of everyone. *Chung* did not mean an absolute

---

[10] Korea was originally called "Choson." In Korean history, there were two Choson dynasties, the first from 2333~108 BC (often referred to as Old Choson) and the second from 1392~1910 AD.

and unconditional obedience to the will of the King or the ruling classes. Throughout many generations and dynasties, loyal subjects did not hesitate to offer frank and honest counsel when the King was in the wrong. It was in the interests of the country to do so, even though it may have caused him displeasure and resulted in unjust consequences to themselves.

Chung was not a concept that was imposed upon the lower classes by the aristocracy, as a means of coercing them into obedience. Rather, it was a practice that began, out of necessity, with the leaders of society. Whether in the curriculums of great educational institutions or the government examinations undergone by public officials, *Chung* formed a fundamental part of an aristocrat's training, and it was a belief that was held to be as important for the upper classes as for the lower. Kings such as Sejong the Great (1397~1450) were an excellent example of this in practice. Sejong lived in a thatch-roofed house, and dressed in worn and patched clothing when not attending to his official duties. During the times of famine, he went without meals in order to feel the pain that his people had to endure. Prime Minister Hwang Hee, who served King Sejong for over thirty years, also lived a life of extreme simplicity, inhabiting a plain and humble dwelling, and going through winter with only a single set of clothes.

The virtue of *Chung* became most apparent during times of national crisis, such as when the country was invaded. For example, Koguryo, one of the ancient kingdoms of Korea, was on one occasion by itself able to repel an invading army of 3.3 million men from Sui China. Later, also, the *Hwarangs* of Silla would contribute to ending the conflict between the three kingdoms and establishing a single nation. Again, when Japan suddenly invaded in 1592, countless soldiers in the "righteous army" (volunteer corps) sacrificed their lives in order to protect the country. But for the patriotism and loyalty of these people, it would not have been possible for Korea to preserve 5,000 years of history and culture.

Chung is in essence love for humanity – the spirit of compassion that has the ability to eradicate the sufferings of the nation, and allows the people to enjoy a life of peace and happiness.

Chapter 3
Wuae: Fraternal Love

Blossoms, Birds, and Puppies

Painted by Yi Am, 16th century, Samsung Museum of Art

The Story of the Good Brothers

In the closing days of the Koryo Dynasty (918~1392), there were two brothers named Yi Songman and Yi Soon, who lived in Taehung village, Chungchong Province. Because the brothers loved each other dearly, they always shared everything, not even holding back the tiniest morsel of food[11]. Even after they married, the two brothers continued to eat their meals at the same table, having breakfast at the older brother Songman's house, and dinner at the house of the younger Soon.

One fall, after the rice crop had been gathered in, the brothers shared the year's harvest equally between them. Later on that night, Soon thought to himself, "Now that I reflect on it, I feel that I have wronged my brother. Since his family is bigger than mine, I should have given him a larger share." He therefore returned to the field where the rice was being kept, and without anyone knowing, took some of his own rice bags and moved them to the pile of his elder brother. When he felt that he had given a fair amount, he returned home.

That same night, Songman also considered what had happened that day, thinking to himself, "Since my brother married only recently, he must be in need of many things." He too went back to the field and moved a number of his own bags to his younger brother's pile. "Will this do?" he wondered. Because it was dark, there was no way of telling, but he felt he had given him enough and

---

[11] Food in those days was much harder to obtain, so sharing was even more important than it is today.

returned home.

The next day, the two brothers thought it very strange that their piles had not grown smaller, but remained the same size. When night came on, the brothers did the same as they had done the night before, and on the next day also, each had as much as on the previous day.

"How strange!" both thought, "For two nights in a row I have tried to give rice to my brother, and yet nothing has changed."

On the third night, each brother again took up several bags of rice on his back, and headed towards the other's field.

On a quiet road, bathed in the gentle radiance of the moon, the two brothers met.

"Who is that?"

"Is that you, Songman?"

"Soon," Songman replied, "Where are you going so late at night?"

When the two brothers saw the sacks of rice they were carrying, they realized what had happened, and embraced each other in tears.

In the sky above, the moon also shed silver tears upon the brothers as it silently observed the happy scene.

More Precious than Gold

From early childhood, Yi Oknyon, a Kaesung governor of the late Koryo Dynasty (918~1392), was very close to his younger brother Yi Chonyon.

One day, the two brothers were walking along a road when they came upon some lumps of gold lying on the bank of the Han River, and decided to share them. Then they boarded a ferry to cross the river, and when they were about midway, Yi Oknyon's younger brother suddenly threw his gold into the water.

The older brother, in shock, asked, "Why did you throw it overboard?"

He answered, "Although I knew the gold was precious, I know that our kinship is even more precious. After we found the gold, the wicked thought occurred to me that if you had not been there, I could have kept the gold all for myself. I was afraid that this jealousy might harm our kinship, and so I threw my gold into the river."

Oknyon, upon hearing his younger brother's words, agreed with him and threw his share into the river as well.

Since then, that branch of the Han River was called "Tu Kum Tan," meaning "the stream where gold was thrown away."

Hungbu and Nolbu[12]

One spring day, the wife and children of a poor man named Hungbu went out to the fields to gather wild vegetables. Hungbu's little son, who was chewing on the roots of a potherb, said that he was hungry, and his mother tried to soothe him by saying, "I will make you a delicious porridge with this shoot. Please be patient." But even as she said this, she knew that their stores of barley and millet had disappeared long ago, and she would only be able to boil the shoot by itself. So she went over to the field where her husband Hungbu was working, and asked him, "Hungbu, please go to your brother's house and ask if he has some grains or anything else to spare, so that I can make our children some vegetable porridge." Hungbu agreed to go, but was doubtful if his elder brother would lend him anything.

Hungbu's brother Nolbu was the richest man in the neighborhood and the owner of many fields and rice paddies. He lived in a big, luxurious tile-roofed house, and kept many servants. But because he was greedy and hard-hearted, many had turned their backs on him.

When Hungbu entered the courtyard of his brother's house, he found Nolbu sitting on the raised floor, smoking a pipe.

"*Hyongnim*[13]," he said, "For some time now my family has had no food, and the children have been starving. Will you please lend me a sack of millet?"

---

[12] The story of Hungbu and Nolbu has been passed down over many generations, and is one of the most famous children's stories in Korea.

[13] This expression, literally meaning "elder brother," is commonly used as an honorific term of address in Korean society.

Although he found it difficult, Hungbu forced himself to ask this favor from his brother. Nolbu, however, rapped his pipe on the tray in front of him and shouted,

"Why, you little thief! What is an able-bodied man in full health doing begging for food? Have you come here just to tell me that you can't earn a living with your own hands? Get out!"

"*Hyongnim*," Hungbu said, "because it is early spring now, there is no work in the fields for laborers[14]. My children are in tears because of their hunger, yet I have nothing to give them, and so I came to you. Please have pity and lend a little food."

Hungbu persisted in asking his brother for help, enduring his harsh words as best he could, but Nolbu slammed the door shut and disappeared inside the house. He then ordered a servant to throw his brother out of the gates.

Having been driven away, Hungbu's shoulders sagged, and he was filled with anxiety. He then began to wonder if he really was a lazy man after all, even though he worked hard every day from morning till night. The true reason for his poverty was in fact his brother Nolbu, who had taken all the estate left by their father and given nothing to his younger sibling.

Seeing her husband return empty-handed, his wife let out a long sigh and began to boil the shoots. Even though it was not porridge with grains as they had been promised, the children rushed to eat it because they were so hungry. It was still several months before the barley was due to be harvested, and Hungbu and his wife were worried about how they would survive until then.

At that moment, they heard a bird singing outside. They opened the door and found a swallow carrying straw and mud in its beak to build a nest under the eaves of their shabby, thatched cottage. Hungbu said quietly to himself, "Alas, little friend, you should have made your nest under the fine, tiled roof of

---

[14] The nobility and wealthy farmers hired laborers in summer and fall, when there was much work to be done in the fields. For those who did not have their own land, therefore, it was often difficult to find employment in winter and early spring.

my brother."

A few days later, five baby swallows were born beneath the eaves of Hungbu's cottage. The mother swallow busied herself catching insects to feed her babies, and Hungbu's family took pleasure in watching the baby swallows grow up.

One day, when Hungbu came back from the fields, he saw a huge serpent on the roof of his house thrusting its head into the swallow's nest. Taken aback, he fetched a long stick and hit the serpent hard, driving it away. He thought that perhaps the serpent had devoured all the birds, for he could not see any baby swallows inside the nest. Feeling sorrow and pity for them, Hungbu was about to sit down in despair, when he noticed a baby swallow which had fallen in the front yard, fluttering its wings.

As Hungbu held it in his hands, he found that the poor creature had broken its leg. His wife and children gathered round. They bandaged the swallow's leg, and placed it back inside the nest with great care. Hoping that the baby swallow would recover, Hungbu and his family looked inside the nest every day and fed the bird with small insects as its mother had done. After some time had passed, the baby swallow's leg healed, and it could fly as well as any other bird. As fall began to draw near, the swallow flew away to the warm lands of the south.

Winter passed, and spring arrived. One day, as Hungbu was making straw sandals in the front yard, a swallow appeared in the sky and began to circle above his head. It dropped something in front of him, and when he picked it up, he realized it was a gourd seed. Hungbu was puzzled, but planted the seed beneath the wall near his house. The very next morning, to his amazement, he found that it had already sprouted and was showing above the ground. He and his wife marveled at the extraordinary sight.

By day and by night, the seedling continued to grow, and soon the whole of Hungbu's thatched cottage was covered with its lush vines and leaves. Huge, round gourds later appeared, and were soon ripe and hard. Thinking they would eat the insides of the gourds and dry the shells to use them as bowls, Hungbu gathered the ripe gourds down from the vine branches, and he and his wife began to saw them open, singing,

"Saw it open, saw it open

Eat the fruit and dry the shell

Praise the Heavens for their kindness

Saw it open, saw it well!"

As the two were singing, the gourd split open and grains of rice poured out. Stunned, they quickly began to gather them up.

"Hungbu, this must surely be a dream," said his wife, wild with happiness.

"The Heavens really are trying to help us!" Hungbu replied, "Otherwise, how could rice come out of a gourd?"

Then they began to saw open another, and this time found money inside. They were astonished.

"Hungbu," said his wife, "I'm sure this money doesn't belong to someone else. Let's put it quickly into a bag."

"Dearest," Hungbu exclaimed, "Now we are rich!" The husband and wife danced for joy.

When the children returned from the fields, their eyes opened wide with amazement. The whole family gathered round, their faces all smiling for the first time in years. They began to open another gourd, wondering what they would find inside. When the third gourd opened, a beautiful angel came out. This surprised them even more, and Hungbu thought to himself, "Perhaps this lady is the owner of the rice and the money in the other two gourds. I have taken them as if they were my own! What shall I do?"

The beautiful angel bowed to Hungbu and his family, and then spoke to the remaining two gourds, "Out, red bottle!" At this command, the first gourd split in half, and a red bottle came out. Then the angel said, "Out, blue bottle!" and the other gourd opened to reveal a blue bottle. The angel then addressed the red and blue bottles, "Now, build a beautiful house for these kind people."

Out of the red bottle, to the ever increasing astonishment of Hungbu and his family, there came many builders, and out of the blue bottle came timber and roof-tiles. The new house was built in no time, and when it was complete, the angel said to Hungbu, "For many years you have endured great hardship, but from now on, please live here in comfort. All this you receive for the grace and charity you showed towards the young swallow." With these words, she vanished. Grateful beyond measure, Hungbu's family bowed down deeply.

Elder brother Nolbu came running when he heard the news. He saw that the old cottage had disappeared, and there now stood in its place a palace fit for a king. He was jealous, and entering the gates, cried out,

"You thief! Tell me the truth right now. By what criminal means have you become so rich overnight?"

"*Hyongnim*," Hungbu replied, "all I did was to mend a swallow's leg," and then told him everything that had happened. Nolbu nodded his head in reply, and asked,

"Since you now have more than I do, may I have some of your great wealth?"

"Yes, *Hyongnim*," Hungbu replied, "Please take whatever you wish."

Choosing an ornate bureau to take home with him, Nolbu left muttering to himself "I'll see for myself if what you have said is true, brother." As soon as he returned, he lay in wait for a swallow to land near him. A few days later, a pair of swallows built a nest in a nearby tree and laid their eggs there. Nolbu was pleased, and waited for a baby swallow to emerge from its egg. When one hatched a few days later, Nolbu could wait no longer. He climbed up the ladder, broke the swallow's leg, and then put on a bandage. The baby swallow survived the ordeal, and flew back to the warm south in the following fall. Nolbu eagerly anticipated the spring, and when it came, he waited for the swallow to return with a seed.

One day, a swallow did appear, and dropped a gourd seed in front of him.

"Wife, wife!" Nolbu shouted excitedly, "Come and see, a blessing from the south!" His wife came running out into the front yard, delighted. They planted the gourd seed under a wall, and reveled in the thought that they would soon be as rich as Hungbu's household.

The gourd seed Nolbu had planted sprouted almost immediately. Its vines soon reached up to the roof of his house, and bore huge gourds. Elated, Nolbu and his wife began to saw open a ripe gourd.

"Saw it open, saw it open,

What lies hidden in the shell?

Bars of gold and princely treasures

Saw it open, saw it well!"

In high spirits, the husband and wife sawed through the gourd. As it opened, a yellowish-gold substance poured out – but it was dung, not gold.

"What on earth is this? What a stench!" they cried, holding their noses and running about frantically in an attempt to escape the flowing dung and its foul smell.

"What is the meaning of this? We expected gold, not this awful filth!"

"Perhaps we chose the wrong gourd," his wife suggested, "Let's try another one."

They began to saw open another gourd. This time, even before they had finished sawing, the gourd split in half and a fearsome-looking goblin came out.

"Nolbu you scoundrel! You treat your younger brother with meanness and injustice, and now, to satisfy your own greed, you have broken the leg of a blameless swallow as well? Have a taste of my club, and learn a few lessons!" With these words, the goblin began to beat him with the club, as Nolbu begged repeatedly for the goblin to spare him. But the goblin turned to the other gourds and shouted, "Come out everyone, let's pull down Nolbu's house!"

The gourds all burst open, and more goblins came out. They pulled the house down, broke it to pieces, and then built a shabby-looking cottage in its place, before disappearing altogether.

Hearing the news, Hungbu and his wife came running to help. Seeing Nolbu and his wife lying unconscious, Hungbu shouted "*Hyongnim*, please wake up!" Together they raised them and took them back to their house.

"*Hyongnim*," Hungbu said to his brother when he awakened, "Do not worry about your house. Please come and live with us."

Hearing Hungbu's kind words, Nolbu finally realized how shamefully he had lived his life, and repented. He held his younger brother's hands and lowered his head in shame.

"Hungbu," he stammered, as the tears rolled down his cheeks, "I am to blame for everything. Please forgive the person who has wronged and hurt you so much."

Afterwards, Nolbu became a good man, and he and his brother lived together happily and in peace.

Chapter 4

Ye: A Virtuous Way of Life

Okchon (Stream of Jade) Bridge of Changgyong Palace

The Origin of *Dubu* and *Kimchi*

In ancient times, there lived a young spiritual practitioner, who attended an enlightened master. The young practitioner cared for the needs of the enlightened master with great devotion, preparing meals for him, farming the land, gathering fruits from the mountains, and collecting firewood.

By the time the enlightened master had reached the age of eighty, he could no longer eat properly because of his bad teeth. The young practitioner's sole concern was to serve his master well, and seeing him unable to eat anything but porridge for several years, he grew perplexed. He began to wonder what he could do to provide his master with better food.

One day, instead of serving him porridge as usual, he served his teacher steamed rice that he had chewed beforehand. However, as he chewed the rice, its sweetness was lost, and he felt sorry that he could not give the rice to his master in its wholeness.

Again, he pondered on whether there was any nutritious food that his teacher would be able to eat easily. He knew that the soy bean was full of nutrition, so he boiled soy beans, pounded them up and pressed them together to create a soft and delicious food. The food he created was *dubu* (*tofu* in Japanese), the health food which is popular today.

In a later period, there lived another enlightened master who was also served by a young practitioner. The young spiritual practitioner had only one thought in his mind, "What can I do for the enlightened master so that he can plant even greater merit before Buddha and the Heavens?"

He thought deeply about how the enlightened master might eat well so that he could maintain his health. The young spiritual practitioner was aware that the radish is a very nutritious vegetable. One spring day, he mixed various vegetables together in a flavored sauce. He then cut a radish into thin slices, soaked them in water, and added salt, letting flower petals float upon the water. When he ate it, the radish tasted too sharp and bitter. He tried salting the radish itself, but still it did not taste very good.

He persevered, however, and at last conceived the idea of putting the salted radish into an earthen jar and allowing it to ferment for a while. This way, the radish was preserved by the salt, and was able to ferment inside the jar. When he took it out and ate it, it tasted good. This is how *kimchi* was first made.

Kimchi has been indispensable to Koreans over the thousands of years since it was created. As a fermented food that is low in fat but rich in vitamins and fiber, and also contains probiotics, it has received much attention from people all over the world for its health benefits.

Dubu and *kimchi*, dishes based on the nutritious soy bean and radish, were created out of the deep reverence of young spiritual practitioners, who served their teachers with all their mind and body.

Kim Jip and Yi Yulgok

Kim Jip (1574~1656) was among the foremost Neo-Confucian scholars during the reign of the Choson ruler King Hyojong. He was also a student of the great scholar Yulgok.

One day, a friend came to Yulgok with a request.

"As you know," he said, "my daughter suffers from a mental disorder and is retarded. It would be impossible for an ordinary person to marry her, and only a saint or an enlightened master would be able to live as her husband. If you know of such a person among your students, please introduce him to me."

After listening to his friend's heartfelt plea, Yulgok thought deeply about the matter for a few days. Then, one morning, he said to his students, "Do not bring food with you tomorrow. I will provide lunch for you myself."

The students were all excited that their teacher had said he would prepare lunch for them. The next day, however, when they saw what had been prepared, they were very disappointed, as the meal consisted only of bitter vegetable soup and steamed barley.

Because Yulgok's students were all from well-to-do families, none of them had ever tasted such things before. While most of the students could not bring themselves to touch the food, one young man finished all that he had been given. The young scholar was Kim Jip.

Yulgok asked him, "Everyone says that the food is too bitter to eat. Did it not taste so to you?"

Kim Jip respectfully replied.

"The food was bitter to my taste also. But I could not bear to leave behind the precious food provided by my teacher, so I ate it all."

Hearing this, Yulgok realized that Kim Jip was a person of rare character. He explained to him that there was a maiden who suffered from mental retardation, and that if he were to marry her, it would be an opportunity for him to cultivate his mind and noble character further.

During this period, people respected the words of their teachers and followed them with absolute faith, for teachers were regarded as one's spiritual parents. Kim Jip, therefore, followed Yulgok's recommendation and married the daughter of his friend.

One day, several years later, Kim Jip and his household were holding a ceremony for their ancestors, and had prepared various offerings of food for them. When the ceremony was about to begin, Kim Jip's wife approached him and began to tug on his sleeve, like a child, asking him to give her some dates to eat.

Kim Jip quickly took a handful of dates from the offerings prepared for the ancestors, and gave them to his wife.

In those days, ancestral rites were very serious events indeed, and performed with great solemnity. The participants would even bathe before the ceremony, in order to purify themselves. Since this incident happened while they were preparing for the offering itself, the elders of the family all reprimanded Kim Jip.

"You are a scholar, and respected by this country's nobility. How could you give food to your wife before offering it to the ancestors?"

Kim Jip replied, "I am aware that the act was an improper one. However, we are holding this occasion in honor of our ancestors, and in order for our ancestors to be happy, our family must be in harmony. If my wife started to cry, or flew into a rage because I refused to give her some dates, this would surely anger the ancestors visiting us on this special occasion. That is why I quickly gave them to her. This whole situation has arisen because of my lack of virtue. Please forgive us."

After listening to Kim Jip's reasoning, all the elders were impressed by his prudence and wisdom.

Later he became Minister of the Interior, and in his old age, made a significant contribution to literature, compiling the *Studies of Korean Courtesy*.

The Hundred Patches Scholar

Fifteen hundred years ago, during the reign of the Silla King Chabi, there lived a virtuous scholar near the Namsan Mountain in the city of Kyongju.

Because he was humble in his wants and always thrifty, he wore clothes that were patched with hemp cloth in many places. There were times when his clothes were patched with over a hundred pieces of hemp cloth. Because of this, people called him the *Paekgyol Sonsaeng*, or "Hundred Patches Scholar."

He was not the least ashamed of his poverty, nor did he complain about it. He possessed a *komungo*, or six-stringed musical instrument, which he always carried with him wherever he went so that he could play music for people. As he played, he would put them at ease and help them to forget their sadness and hardships.

Once, on the final day of the year, the whole town was bustling with the sound of people preparing steamed rice and rice cakes. The scholar's wife, quietly listening to them, said with a sigh,

"Our neighbors are all busily milling rice to prepare for the New Year's celebrations, but we do not have a single grain. How are we to celebrate the New Year?"

Hearing his wife's complaint, Paekgyol began to laugh.

"My dear," he said, "Life and death depend on fate, and poverty and wealth on the Heavens. Therefore, whether wealth or poverty comes to us, we cannot prevent it. And if they leave us, we cannot chase after them. So, what is there to be sad about? Come, I will cheer you up with music."

He then started to play the *komungo*. The music he played had never been heard before. It was like the sound of milling after a good season's harvest. After listening to the joyful tune of *komungo*, his wife felt all her worries melting away.

The cheerful Korean folk tune, "Pang-ah Taryong (Song of Milling)," has been passed down to this day.

The Lands of Bok Changhan

Kwon Supyong was a civil minister from Andong during the Koryo Dynasty (918~1392). His appearance was noble and handsome, and his character gentle and sincere. A diligent scholar, he passed the state examination at an early age, but he was nonetheless a poor man.

When he was serving as a junior officer, a man named Bok Changhan was exiled on uncertain evidence. When Bok left for exile, the state awarded his lands to Kwon, as well as the right to keep the crops produced by his land.

Several years later, Bok was recalled from exile, and he returned to serve in an official role. Bok and Kwon were barely acquainted, but when he heard of his return, Kwon compiled an inventory of the crops that had been harvested from Bok's land during his absence, and went to see him.

"I hear that you have returned from exile," he said, "While you were away, I harvested the crops that grew on your land. I would now like to repay you for what I have received."

Bok was moved, but answered, "I was exiled by a judge's verdict, and if you had not received my lands, the state would have given them to somebody else. Confiscating a criminal's property and bestowing it upon another government official is the law of this country. You took pity on my situation and I would have been grateful even if you had simply returned my lands to me. But now you are trying to give me the crops which have already been harvested. This is truly without precedent."

Kwon, however, would not be refused, and insisted, "To take advantage of your misfortune and profit from your land would be wrong. How can I call these crops mine when you have returned from exile, after a false accusation against you has been disproved?"

Kwon put the inventory papers in front of Bok and quickly left the room. Bok still felt that he could not accept them, and wanted to give them back to Kwon. So he picked up the papers and threw them out of the door, and then went back inside after locking the gate.

Kwon, after staring at the closed gate for a while, picked up the papers, tied them to a rock and threw them inside Bok's house over the wall by the gate.

Giving Away a Fortune

In the days of the Choson Dynasty (1392~1910), during the reign of King Yongjo, there lived a scholar called Kim Chaehae. He once bought an old house from a certain widow. One day, he was digging in the ground to rebuild a fence that had fallen down, and after he had been at work for a long time, he suddenly hit upon something hard.

He laid down his mattock and began to clear away the earth with his hands. He discovered that a large urn had been buried there. Cautiously he opened the lid, and was surprised to find that it was full of gold.

"What a stroke of good fortune," he exclaimed, "Now I am rich!"

Since he was constantly immersed in study, he was always struggling to make ends meet, and after finding this store of gold he thought that the Heavens were finally showing him kindness. He carefully dug around the urn and lifted it out. Looking at the amount of gold, it seemed to be at least three, or perhaps four times the value of his new house.

However, as he sat before the urn, his mind was filled with unease. Even though it had come from a house that he had bought with own money, it occurred to him that the urn was not his.

Feeling that he had allowed himself to be blinded by greed, the scholar swiftly collected his mind. Coveting the possessions of others was the way of the unwise, he reasoned, and for a wise man the most proper thing to do would be to find the urn's true owner. When he reached this conclusion, he felt much happier. He called his wife and told her everything that had happened, suggesting that they return the gold to the former owner of the house. Without hesitation his wife agreed, and they immediately wrote a letter to the widow who had sold it to them.

Reading the letter, the widow was greatly moved by their honesty. A few days afterwards, she came to visit the house of the scholar and said,

"Even though this gold has come from the grounds of my old house, it must have been buried there for a very long time. How could I hide that truth and claim that it is mine? If it is impossible to find the owner, I suggest that we share it between us."

The scholar's wife replied,

"Thank you, but we cannot accept your kind offer. If we had wanted the gold, we would not have told you in the first place."

Taken aback by this unexpected reply, the widow asked,

"Why do you insist on giving it all to me, even though it is not mine?"

The scholar's wife calmly replied,

"Neither you nor we know who the true owner is. However, whereas I have a husband, and am able to run our household without much difficulty, you have to make a living and keep a house all by yourself. This is a truly difficult task. Therefore, please take the gold yourself."

With these words, the scholar's wife gave the widow the urn. Grateful and embarrassed, the widow did not know what to do. As the scholar's wife was behaving as if it were perfectly natural for her to receive the gold, she could find no words to say in reply. She took the urn back home, and never afterwards forgot their kindness.

True Wealth

A life of purity and simplicity, free from the pursuit of material wealth, was an ideal taught by the ancient sages, and the guiding philosophy of the Korean *sunbi*[15]. It was the practice of the *sunbi* to strive harder for a life of purity and frugality as their social status rose. When their position in the government increased by one degree, they would reduce the number of rooms in their houses by one, have one fewer side-dish at meals, and would not have any new clothes made that year.

The mode of living pursued by the *sunbi* was grounded in the Ten Necessities (Kor. *Sip Yo*). According to this rule, a *sunbi* should have no more than the following: a shelf of books, a set of *komungo*[16], a friend, a pair of shoes, a pillow, a paper window, a brazier, a wooden veranda, a walking stick, and a mule. This gives us an insight into the life and spirit of the *sunbi*, who knew how to enjoy spiritual wealth over material wealth.

Sang Yongbu of Imchon town was a wealthy man, who won great admiration by his virtuous practice of lending money to those who found themselves in sudden need of it. On the last day of every year, he would take all the promissory notes from his safe, on which were written the details of his

---

[15] *Sunbi* refers to a learned person of nobility and integrity. The *Sunbi* were a class in Korean society who were able to engage in scholarly pursuits and become public officials. While similar in certain respects to the *Samurai* of Japan, the main difference between them was that *Samurai* were a class of warriors whereas *Sunbi* were a class of scholars.

[16] *Komungo* is a traditional Korean stringed musical instrument. Confucian scholars used it as a means of cultivating the mind.

debtors' houses, and burn them in the yard outside his house. He took great delight in watching the smoke from the crackling papers rise into the sky. Many people said that his descendants would prosper because of his virtuous deeds, and indeed his grandson, Sang Chin, became a well-respected prime minister during the reign of King Myongjong.

Many *sunbi* scholars would burn records of money owed to them on the last day of the year. In particular, it was customary to write off debts that had been unpaid for over three years due to the debtor's ongoing financial difficulties. It was thought that if one tried to make excessive profit out of items that were needed by others for survival, such as a house, food, and clothes, one would invariably be punished with misfortune.

According to the belief that a life of purity and giving brings good fortune, while a life of greed and selfishness brings the opposite, the pure, simple life was the truest form of wealth for the *sunbi* of Korea.

A Compassionate Gentleman

During the reign of King Sejong the Great, Yoon Hwae (1380~1436) served as Vice-minister of the *Chiphyonjon* (Royal Institute of Research) and Minister of Literacy and Art, and was considered the most accomplished writer of poetry and prose of his day. He was often personally called upon by the King.

One day when he was young, Yoon was traveling in the countryside, and stopped at an inn when it began to grow dark. However, the inn's owner had no rooms vacant and could not take him in.

Left with no choice, Yoon settled underneath the low eaves of a house and spent the night there. From this vantage point, he happened to witness the daughter of the innkeeper come out and drop a large pearl in the yard. At that moment, a duck that was passing by quickly came over and swallowed it, thinking it was food of some kind.

When the owner of the inn found that the pearl was missing, he was suspicious of Yoon Hwae. He bound him with rope and decided to take him to the local court on the following day to prosecute him. Yoon did not try to defend or explain himself, but only requested that the owner tie the duck next to him.

The next morning, the owner came outside to take him away. With a calm expression on his face, Yoon told him to view the duck's excrement.

He thought this strange but proceeded to look, and found his daughter's pearl embedded there. Surprised, he said in an apologetic voice, "Why did you not say anything about this last night? Then all of this could have been avoided."

Yoon smiled quietly and said, "If I had told you last night, you would have undoubtedly cut the duck open in order to find the pearl."

The owner was embarrassed and could not reply.

Secret Giving

During the reign of King Wonjong (r.1259~1274) of the Koryo dynasty, there lived a man named Yoon Sung. Nearby his house, there dwelt a poor, low-ranking official.

One evening, Yoon was about to retire when he heard a strange noise outside. He put away his sleeping blankets, and made his way towards where the noise was coming from. In his garden, he encountered a strange sight: the poor official who lived nearby was stuck in a hole in the fence, and was squirming about, trying to free himself.

As Yoon walked towards him, he asked,

"Why are you here? What have you come for?"

The man stopped struggling and confessed,

"The truth is that our household has run out of food and I came to this house in order to steal a sack of grain. I made a hole in the fence and found the storehouse, but on my way out I discovered that the hole was too small, and now I am stuck. Please, forgive me."

Yoon then pushed the man through the hole in the fence. Overcome with embarrassment, the official tried to run away. Yoon chased after him and caught him. He gave him the sack of rice he had left behind and said,

"You are in this situation because you were hungry, and you have done nothing wrong. Since the people in my household do not know of this, take the sack of grain you have from my storehouse. All this will remain a secret between us."

Greatly moved by his compassion, the poor official knelt before him and thanked him deeply. With tears in his eyes, he walked away with the sack of grain on his back.

Yoon kept his word and did not tell his family about the incident. When it was discovered that a sack of rice was missing, they assumed it was the work of a thief and left it at that.

Some time later, the official received his salary. Bringing rice wine and other delicacies as gifts, he came to Yoon and tearfully offered his sincere thanks.

Pukchon-daek of Hahwe Village

In the South Eastern part of the Korean peninsula, there is a village called Hahwe. It is a peaceful town of quaint tile-roofed houses and thatched huts, located between the range of hills that extends from Mount Taebak. The Nakdong River gracefully curves around it on its way to the sea. This serene and beautiful town is often referred to as "The Town of Nobility," as it has produced many high-ranking officials, such as Prime Minister Ryu Songryong.

There are many historic houses in the village of Hahwe, but "Pukchon-daek" (literally "House of the Northern Village") is thought to be one of the most beautiful traditional houses in all Korea. The house is the biggest in the village, occupying approximately two acres of land, and containing 72 rooms in total. Its household has enjoyed wealth and renown for over seven generations.

The house originally became famous in the neighboring area after a flood that occurred there in the summer of 1859. One night, a ferry boat that was carrying people to the town of Hahwe from across the river for a funeral service was overturned in the flood.

During that time, there were no flash lights or street lamps, and the area was completely dark. The people who fell into the river were screaming for help, but there were no boats nearby to rescue them.

Fortunately, there were piles of well dried *Chunyang* (a variety of pine tree grown in the mountains of Kangwon Province) stacked beside the river. Ryu Tosong, who was the governor of Kyongsang Province, had been drying them for three years in order to build a tile-roofed house with them. Since *Chunyang* trees usually grow straight and do not become gnarled, they were useful for building such houses.

In order to save the people, Ryu threw the *Chunyang* wood into the river for them to cling on to. When he had thrown enough wood into the river, the remaining timbers were used as firewood to provide light and warmth for the survivors. Many lives were saved as a result of his efforts.

Later on, with much difficulty, Ryu was able to replace the *Chunyang* lumber he had lost. After he had left the timbers to dry for another three years, the house was finally built. The house was called "Pukchon-daek" and remains there to this day. Even after 150 years, his descendants are more proud of Ryu's generous spirit than the tile-roofed house he built.

The Rice Chest of Wunjoru

In Kurye city, Cholla Province, there is a house built by Yu Yiju (1726~1797) who served as governor there during the reign of King Youngjo. The house is called "Wunjoru," which literally means "House of a Bird Hiding in the Clouds."

In this house there is a rice chest that has been passed down from generation to generation. It is a cylindrical chest, made from a hollowed-out log. On the underside of the chest there is a small rectangular hole (5cm x 10cm), and an inscription "For anyone and everyone" carved on the stopper. Its meaning is that anyone can freely take rice from the chest.

The Yu family used the rice chest to help needy people in the area. Travellers who were passing through would also take rice from the chest. In order to protect the dignity of the people who used it, they put the chest far away from the main building so that people would not run into the owners.

The chest can hold up to two and a half sacks of rice (200 kg). When the stopper with the inscription is turned, the rice comes out through the hole at the bottom. The quantity of rice taken by each person was normally around two to four liters. People rarely took more than this, even though the owners were not there to see them.

The Wunjoru held close to twenty acres of rice paddies, which produced 200 sacks of rice every year. Since 36 of those sacks of rice went into the rice chest, the Yu family gave away almost a fifth of their total produce to people who were in need.

The owner of the household checked the contents of the rice chest each month. If there was ever any rice left over, he would always tell his daughter in law, "We have to practice the virtue of giving for our family to prosper. Give this rice to neighbors who are in need of it immediately. Make sure that there is no rice left in the chest at the end of the month."

The Kurye area was notorious for the many peasant uprisings that took place in it towards the end of Choson period, and also for guerilla warfare during the Korean War. There is no doubt that the Wunjoru house was able to survive the tumultuous history of the region because of the benevolent spirit behind this rice chest, which had warmed the hearts of many people.

Kim Manduk: Jeju Island's "Lady of Virtue"

Kim Manduk, known as the "Lady of Virtue" of Jeju Island, was born in 1739, the only daughter in a family of five.

Manduk's father was known for his diligence, and was also a shrewd businessman. He was a merchant who traveled back and forth between Jeju and mainland Korea, trading the island's maritime produce, such as seaweed, abalone and oyster, in return for rice from the mainland.

However, in the autumn of the year that Manduk turned eleven, her father ran into a terrible storm at sea, and lost his life. The tragedy of his death proved too great for Manduk's mother to bear, and within a year and a half, she also passed away.

Having lost both her parents at such a young age, Manduk and her brothers were left in the care of their uncle. When his fortunes declined, however, Manduk was sent to an old *kisaeng* (professional entertainer) who noticed her talent for singing, dancing and playing music, and so had her registered as a *kisaeng*. At the time, Korean society was strictly hierarchical, and *kisaengs* belonged to the lowest class. As she grew older and became more aware of how the world perceived her, in spite of her having been born into a respectable family, she hoped to be restored to her former status. She appealed several times to the provincial authorities, but was refused on every occasion. She persevered, however, and eventually managed to meet the Governor of Jeju Island, Sin Kwang-ik, who listened to her plea, and at long last allowed her to be removed from the register of *kisaengs*. Later, at the age of 20, she was married to Ko

Sunheum, but soon after lost her husband to an infectious disease.

Having suffered so many of life's hardships so soon in life, Manduk began to save money and to lead a life of thrift and diligence. Noting the advantages and unique characteristics of Jeju as a harbor city, she set up an inn for traveling merchants near the port. Besides being a place where they could rest, it offered commercial services as well, such as the handling and sale of foreign goods shipped on consignment.

Gifted as she was with a natural talent for business, her inn soon prospered. Drawing upon her experiences as a *kisaeng,* she sold textiles, personal ornaments, cosmetics and the similar wares to the female aristocracy of Jeju island. She also traded in Jeju's own specialties, such as tangerines and the antlers of young deer, selling them on to the mainland. She sought to attract more shipping to the port, eventually possessing a ship of her own. In an age when talented women were often overlooked and even suppressed, the story of her success soon became a common topic of conversation. In spite of her success, she continued to lead a frugal life. Her belief was, "In a year of good harvest, we must prepare for a bad harvest, and save for the future. Those who live in comfort must think of those in need, and live sparingly in gratitude to the Heavens."

In 1794, as Manduk neared her mid-fifties, the whole of Jeju fell under a great famine, as a result of a series of typhoons which battered the island in succession. The Governor of Jeju submitted a request for aid to the Royal Court, stating that the Island had suffered devastating damage as "powerful easterly winds blew on August 27th and 28th, sending roof-tiles flying and stones rolling." In the February of the following year, five ships carrying relief supplies were sunk in a storm, and as Jeju looked forward to a barren spring harvest, death cast a long, grim shadow over the island.

Meanwhile, Manduk thought to herself, "Hasn't all my wealth come from the people of Jeju? What is the use of holding on to my riches if they are all to perish? What benefit would my wealth be then? Since it belonged to the people to begin with, to them it should be returned." She then used her wealth to purchase five hundred sacks of grain. She shared a tenth of these with her relatives and those who had been kind to her, and offered the remaining four hundred and fifty sacks as a general relief for the public.

The Governor of Jeju was very surprised by Manduk's gift. The greatest donations up to this point had been from the former local magistrate Ko Hanlok, who had donated three hundred sacks, and the military official Hong Sampil and the scholar Yang Sungbum, who had given a hundred sacks each. The Governor of Jeju had described Ko Hanlok's contribution as "an astonishing amount," and the King had granted him the special appointment of chief local magistrate, later awarding him the mayorship as well. Hong Sampil and Yang Sungbum were promoted to the Royal Guard in recognition of their gifts. The King was heard to say at the time that "to give a hundred sacks in a land as barren as Jeju is equal to giving a thousand on the mainland." Therefore it was only natural that the Governor should be astounded by Manduk's donation of 450 sacks, by which she exhausted her entire personal fortune. The government of Jeju distributed the rice given by Manduk to the people, according to their level of hardship, and the streets were filled with grateful citizens calling out her name.

In time, news of Manduk's act of charity reached the Royal Court. Such an act of compassion, from one who was not even a member of the aristocracy, greatly moved King Chongjo, who immediately ordered the Governor of Jeju to "carry out any wish the lady Manduk might have, however difficult it is." Hearing this, Manduk made a request which no one expected: "I have no other wish than to visit the capital Seoul and look upon the Palace where our King resides, and to behold the Twelve Thousand Summits of the Kumgang

Mountain[17]."

Although during that time it was forbidden for the women of Jeju to leave the Island, the King willingly granted her wish. He provided a horse for her carriage, and ordered the various provincial governors to tend to her comfort as she made her journey from the south. In 1796, upon her arrival in the capital, the King gave her an official position within the Palace Infirmary, so that she would be able have audience with the King and the Queen (according to the law of that time, commoners could not be granted direct audience with the King). On this occasion, the King said to her, "That you have saved thousands who were suffering from starvation, in a heroic spirit, although a mere woman, is indeed laudable." And with these words, the King bestowed special gifts upon her.

Manduk spent the winter in Seoul that year, and in the following spring traveled to Kumgang Mountain, where she was greeted by the magnificent spectacle of the Twelve Thousand Summits. It was there also that she came across a golden statue of the Buddha, before which she reverently bowed down and offered her respects. At the time there were no Buddhist temples in Jeju, and this was the first time that Manduk had seen a temple and statue of the Buddha.

On her return to Seoul, she visited the Palace again and expressed the wish

---

[17] Mount Kumgang (kumgang = diamond) is considered by many to be one of the most beautiful places in the world. It is particularly famous for the splendor of its 12,000 peaks. Comments on its beauty, from the past up to the present, include: "To be born in Koryo, and to behold the Dimaond Mountain, that is my heart's greatest wish." (A scholar of Northern Song China, 960~1127); "Surely the beauty of that eleven miles is not much exceeded anywhere on earth…" (Isabella Bird, an English explorer, 1890); "Of the six days God spent creating Heaven and Earth, He must have devoted the last day solely to Mt. Kumgang." (Gustaf VI Adolf, King of Sweden, 1926)

to go back to Jeju Island, whereupon the King again presented her with gifts. By this time, Manduk's name had spread far and wide in the capital, and many were seeking her acquaintance, including scholars and nobles of the court. Che Chegong, the Prime Minister, wrote a biography of her, and great scholars of the time such as Pak Chega, Chong Yakyong and Yi Kahwan, all left verses commemorating her deeds – deeds which it would have been difficult for aristocrats, officials, and even the state itself to accomplish.

With all her wishes fulfilled, Manduk returned to Jeju Island. Fifteen years later, in October 1812, she died at the age of 74. According to her wish, she was buried on a mountain which commanded a view of the entire island.

The Province of Jeju has since established the Manduk Award, a yearly prize awarded to a lady of outstanding conduct, in commemoration of the virtue and grace which Manduk bestowed upon her home island.

A Culture of Respect and Benevolence

It is an old tradition in Korea to respect one's elders. Families and towns alike have always had an elderly person as their central figure and leader. Young people, therefore, treated them with respect and always relied on their wisdom when they had to make an important decision.

As this tradition still remains in Korea, young people bow to their elders, use courteous language when speaking to them and also give up their seats for them when riding a bus or a train. When they receive something from an older person, they accept it with both hands, and they also try to behave respectfully when older people are present.

Dutiful care for parents and respect for one's elders may be thought of as a chain of love that connects members of Korean society vertically, whereas *Jeong*, or benevolence, is the tie that links everyone horizontally. These traditions have their roots in the history and culture of Korea, and their longstanding practice is affirmed by records from China. According to the *Shan Hai Jing* (山海經), one of China's oldest geographical works, "Koreans always act in a conciliatory manner and do not quarrel with one another"; "always sit decorously and do not try to harm others"; "respect one another and refrain from criticism"; and "do not hesitate to sacrifice themselves to help others who are in danger." Dong Fang Shuo (東方朔), a well known scholar of the Chinese Han Dynasty, commented on the honest nature of the Korean people, saying, "At first glance, they appear to be very naïve, but in truth this is kind-heartedness." (神異經)

The culture of *Jeong*, or treating others as if they were one's own family, has made a strong impression on the minds of visitors to the country. Claude-Charles Dallet, a French missionary to Korea during the late Choson Dynasty, wrote about the culture of *Jeong* in his book, *A History of Korean Catholicism*:

> Whether it is a complete stranger or an acquaintance, Koreans consider it a shame and a great offense to refuse to serve a meal to someone who visits during a meal time. Usually, even the poor farmers having their lunch by the roadside will be the first to offer to share their meal with a passer-by. If there is a small party or a celebration, it is expected that all the neighbors will be invited. If a person without much wealth needs to travel to a distant place to visit his friends or family, he need not take long to prepare for his trip. All he has to do is carry his walking stick, a pipe, and a small sack with some clothes on his shoulder, with some money if he has any, and his room and board will be taken care of by people's benevolence. At night, he need not find an inn. He merely has to go to a household that keeps its guest rooms open to all travelers, and he will find shelter and food for the night. At meal times, he will definitely be served a meal. If he is too tired, or weather conditions are not favorable, he may stay for one or two extra days, and no one would claim that he was taking advantage of his host's hospitality.

Because this network of *Jeong* linked everyone throughout Korea and dissolved selfish motives for personal gain, Koreans could live in harmony and good humor even amidst difficult economic conditions. In another part of *A History of Korean Catholicism*, Dallet writes:

For important events such as weddings and funerals, each person believes that it is his or her duty to help. Everyone brings a gift and provides whatever assistance they can. Some will be in charge of buying groceries, and others will be in charge of preparing for the ceremony. Poor neighbors who cannot contribute money will volunteer to announce the event to other neighbors, or relatives living far away, or will stay up all night to provide the necessary labor. It is as if they were all volunteering for a public endeavor of the highest importance and not a private event. If someone's house is destroyed as a result of a disaster such as a fire or a flood, his neighbors will supply the labor and material in order to rebuild the house. His neighbors will rush to the site with supplies of stones, logs, and thatch. They will also volunteer to provide two or three days of labor for the actual building of the house. If someone moves from one town to another, everyone in the new town will work together to build a small house for him. If someone travels to a distant mountain to cut trees or make charcoal, all he needs to do is take some rice with him. The people of the town he travels to will prepare his meal and provide side dishes for him as well. When someone becomes ill, anyone who has the appropriate medicine will give it to him for free, without being asked for it. Usually, people will rush to give the medicine, but they will refuse to be paid for it. They will always lend their farming tools to people who need them. They will even lend their cows for farming unless it is a busy farming season.

Dallet said that any Westerner who witnessed these things would wonder why Koreans act in such a way. Since the early days of Old Choson, some five thousand years ago, many enlightened teachers lived and taught in Korea. These enlightened masters educated people in many ways, directly and indirectly, teaching them to practice kindness and compassion towards others. This teaching was the same in spirit as the doctrine of Tangun, the founding father of Old Choson, who said that one should "live and act for the benefit of all mankind (Kor. *Hongik Ingan*)." The people's minds were purified by these teachings, and their hearts became warm and generous.

This Korean culture of living together selflessly went beyond human society and extended to nature as well. In the small towns of Korea, it was common during autumn to see persimmon trees with six or seven persimmons left unpicked. These remaining fruits were called the "magpie feast" and were left for birds that might need them during the deep winter, when food was scarce. Also, in spring, when people picked wild vegetables known to be enjoyed by pheasants, they always buried some beans close by, so that the pheasants could feed on them. These customs originated from the ancient sages and enlightened masters, who taught people to treat everyone, including animals, with kindness. Over many generations, such beliefs became deeply rooted in the traditions and customs of Korea.

Unfortunately, the culture and values of *Jeong* have been disappearing in the rapid modernization of the past few decades. Protecting and sharing with the world the precious traditions that have built up and been passed down over thousands of years is probably the highest form of respect that Koreans today can show to their ancestors who began them.

Bibliography

Samguk Sagi (History of the Three Kingdoms)
Samguk Yusa (Memorabilia of the Three Kingdoms)

Bahn, Jaesik. *Hyohaeng Baekseon* (A Hundred Selected Stories of Hyo), Seoul: Baek Jung Dang, 2004.

Jo, Yongheon. *Jo Yong-heon Salon*, Seoul: Random House, 2006.

Kim, Jaewoong, *Momunun Ba Upsi Maumul Naera*, Pohang: Yong Hwa, 1992.

Pak, Younggyu. *Koguryosa Yiyagi* (History of Koguryo), Paju: Kim Yong Sa, 2006.

Ryeo, Jeoungdong. *Hyodo Bogam* (Korean Good-Son), Seoul: Muneoumsa, 1997.

Seondo Culture Research Center. *Hanguk Seondoui Yoksawa Munhwa* (Culture and History of Korean Seondo), Chonan: International Graduate University for Peace Press, 2006.

Sin, Yonwoo, and Yong-ran Sin. *Jewangdului Chaeksa* (Monarchs' Tacticians), Seoul: Baeksung, 2001.

Yi, Gyutae. *Hangukhak Essay* (Essays on Korea), Seoul: Sinwon Munhwasa, 1995.

_____. *Hangukinui Chongsin Munhwa* (Spirit and Culture of Koreans), Seoul: Sinwon Munhwasa, 2000.

Yi, Yongbum. *Saram Doemui Dori Hyo* (A Virtuous Way of life, Hyo), Seoul: Baum, 2004.

_____. *Insaengui Cham Seuseung Sunbi* (True Teachers of Life, Sunbi), 2 volumes, Seoul: Baum, 2004.

Internet Sources

http://www.manduk.org
http://www.nongae.or.kr
http://www.hwarangdo.or.kr
http://www.khrd.or.kr

Recommended Places for Visitors of Korea

Gyeong Bok Gung Palace

Gyeong Bok Gung is a palace located in northern Seoul. It was the main and largest palace of the Choson Dynasty (1392-1910) and one of the Five Grand Palaces built by the Choson monarchs. Today the palace is open to the public, and houses the National Folk Museum of Korea.

▪ (02) 3700-3900   ▪ www.royalpalace.go.kr [Korean, English]

CHANG DEOK GUNG PALACE

Chang Deok Gung is one of the most beautiful places in Korea, and was designated as UNESCO's World Cultural Heritage in December 1997. Chang Deok Gung is devided into administrative quarters, residential quarters, and the rear garden. The rear garden has exquisite pavillions, the court archives, a library, and ponds, all in beautiful harmony with the natural surroundings.

▪ (02) 762-8261   ▪ www.cdg.go.kr [Korean, English, Japanese Chinese]

NATIONAL MUSEUM OF KOREA

A window to the richness of Korean history and culture, the Natioanl Museum of Korea reopened at the heart of the captial city Seoul, on October 20, 2005. With a collection of aver 11,000 works of art, the Natioanl Museum of Korea is the 6th largest museum in the world. The museum is oepn every except Mondays, and no admission fee is required for the permanent exhibits.

▪ (02) 20077-9000   ▪ www.museum.go.kr [Korea, Englsh, Japanese, Chinese]

LEEUM, SAMSUNG MUSEUM OF ART

Leeum, Samsumg Musem of Art in Itaewon, Seoul is a highly recommended place for architecture and art lovers. This beautiful and artfully deisgned museum holds one of the finest collections in the world, ranging from ancient paintings and ceramics of Korea to the modern day contemporary art of the world.

- (02) 2014-6900   ▪ www.leeum.org [Korean, English]

KOREA HOUSE

Korea House is a comprehensive cultural complex representing traditional Korean culture. It introduces traditional court cuisine and stages traditional Korean art including traditional music, dance, plays, ceremonies, and games, and also offers souvenirs that exhibit the distinctive characteristics of the Korean culture.

- (02) 2266-9101~3   ▪ www.koreahouse.or.kr [Korean, English, Japanese, Chinese]

NATIONAL CENTER FOR KOREAN TRADITIONAL PERFORMING ARTS

NCKTPA aims to preserve the numerous art works that have originated from Korea during its history of five thousand years, as well as many East Asian art traditions. Regular performance is held on every Saturday at 17:00.

- (02) 580-3333   ▪ http://www.ncktpa.go.kr [Korean, English]

HWASEONG FORTRESS

Hwaseong Fortress, regarded by UNESCO as the epitome of military architecture, was built by Chong Yak-yong in 1796. Consisting of 48 structures, the castle complex was designed with the utmost care. As well as being beautiful to look at, the castle contains many ingenious defensive features. Traditional military ceremonies are held at every Saturday at 14:00.

- (031) 254335   ▪ http://hs.suwon.ne.kr [Korean, English, Japanese, Chinese]

Editorial Contributors

Lee, Soon-Young is a scholar and educator. He received his bachelor's degree in Law from Dongguk University, a master's degree in Justice Administration from Northeastern University, and an interdisciplinary doctoral degree in Law, Policy and Society from Boston University. He has served as the President of Hanzhong University, Vice-Chairman of the Seoul Metropolitan Board of Education, and Expert Advisor to the Presidential Committee for Globalization. He is currently serves as the Chair Professor of Seoul University of Foreign Studies and the Chairman of the Sung Kyun Kwan (Korean Confucian Institute), the renowned 700 year-old center for Confucian studies and traditional ceremonies.

Lee, Jiseon is the executive editor of Korean Spirit and Culture Series. She graduated in English Language and Literature Department from Ewha Womans University, and studied Literature and Philosophy at Wilson College and Boston College in the United States.

Chang, Hang-Jin is a lawyer at Linklaters LLP in London, specializing in international finance. He majored in Law at Oxford University, and has extensive experience in Korean-English translations.

Han, Yoon-Sang is a lawyer in New York City. He majored in Economics at Wesleyan University and received his law degree from William and Mary School of Law. He has translated various texts from Korean to English, including *Polishing the Diamond, Enlightening the Mind* (Wisdom Publications, 1999).

Jackson, Matthew is a management consultant at Arthur D. Little in London. He majored in Classics at Oxford University, and has worked for many years as an editor of English translations. He regularly writes on Korean issues, in particular the traditional arts and science.

Korean Spirit and Culture Website

www.koreanhero.net

www.kscpp.net

All booklets published in the series are available on our website, as well as additional materials covering various aspects of Korean history and culture.

Published so far:
Admiral Yi Sun-sin
King Sejong the Great
Chung Hyo Ye
Fifty Wonders of Korea
Taste of Korea

Online video library includes:
Korean Cuisine
Hanbok, the Clothes of Nature
Korean Economy: LG, Samsung and Hyundai
UNESCO World Heritage in Korea
And more…